journalism

Geoff Pridmore

TEACH YOURSELF BOOKS

75p

C000132475

For UK orders: please contact Bookpoint Ltd, 39 Milton Park, Abingdon, Oxon OX14 4TD. Telephone: (44) 01235 400414, Fax: (44) 01235 400454. Lines are open from 9.00–6.00, Monday to Saturday, with a 24 hour message answering service. Email address: orders@bookpoint.co.uk

For USA & Canada orders: please contact NTC/Contemporary Publishing, 4255 West Touhy Avenue, Lincolnwood, Illinois 60646–1975, USA. Telephone: (847) 679 5500, Fax: (847) 679 2494.

Long renowned as the authoritative source for self-guided learning – with more than 30 million copies sold worldwide – the *Teach Yourself* series includes over 200 titles in the fields of languages, crafts, hobbies, business and education.

British Library Cataloguing in Publication Data
A catalogue entry for this title is available from The British Library

Library of Congress Catalog Card Number: On file

First published in UK 2000 by Hodder Headline Plc, 338 Euston Road, London, NW1 3BH.

First published in US 2000 by NTC/Contemporary Publishing, 4255 West Touhy Avenue, Lincolnwood (Chicago), Illinois 60646–1975 USA.

The 'Teach Yourself' name and logo are registered trade marks of Hodder & Stoughton Ltd.

Typeset by Transet Limited, Coventry, England.
Printed in Great Britain for Hodder & Stoughton Educational, a division of Hodder Headline Plc, 338 Euston Road, London NW1 3BH by Cox & Wyman Ltd, Reading, Berkshire.

Impression number   10 9 8 7 6 5 4 3 2 1
Year   2005 2004 2003 2002 2001 2000

CONTENTS

PREFACE

Britain produces more newspapers and magazines per head of population than any other country in the world. As a nation, we are spoilt for choice when it comes to daily, weekly and monthly news and information. Our love of news isn't so surprising when you consider that throughout history the British have recorded more information about their daily lives than any other nation. From *Beowulf* and the *Anglo-Saxon Chronicle* to today's web pages, information has been handed down to us through the work of innovators such as William Caxton and Tim Berners-Lee; and in all manner of formats: stories, chronicles, journals, charters, proclamations, speeches, diaries, even confessions.

As inheritors of such an information-rich history, we might be justified in considering ourselves a nation of journalists and consumers of news. If we're not reading newspapers, we're listening to news broadcasts on radio or watching 24-hour news on TV and on the Internet. The national appetite for news is insatiable and so it is hardly any wonder that many aspire to work in news and media.

With that appetite in mind, the aim of this book is to give practical instruction in how to become a journalist and how to work as a journalist. In recent years, few professions have seen such enormous change, as technical innovations and new work practices replace old ones. Journalism is now most commonly entered through further and higher education, but to function properly in the workplace, the journalist requires the same skills as of old: instinct, talent, diplomacy and a lot of common sense. A 'nose for news' is not something that can be acquired overnight. It is either a natural part, or becomes part of a journalist's make-up over time: and it's as necessary today as it was a thousand years ago when a young messenger dashed hotfoot from Hastings with news that changed the English-speaking world.

ACKNOWLEDGEMENTS

A big thank you is in order to:

The current teaching staff and former students at Falmouth College of Art: Bob Benjafield; Adrian Butterworth; Don Deacon; Dennis Gartside; Jim Hall; Caroline Hodgson; Colin Maunder.

To the journalists and others who kindly gave their time to talk to me about their work: Magnus Carter and the team at Mentor Communications Consultancy, Bristol; Daniel Garrett; Alastair Kennedy-Sloane; Major Doreen Cadwallader; Ian Martin; Kate Moseley; Tristan Nichols.

Special thanks to those organizations who kindly, and promptly, sent information on request: Association of European Journalists British Section; Gerald Hine-Haycock at BBC News Training Centre; The Chartered Institute of Journalists; National Council for the Training of Journalists; National Union of Journalists; Periodicals Training Council; The Press Complaints Commission; The Radio Academy; Skillnet SW.

To my friends and colleagues at Open World Ltd for their patience and support.

And finally, to my parents, Alf and Rachel, to whom I dedicate this book.

1 | AN EDUCATION IN JOURNALISM

The media industries no longer provide comprehensive basic training for trainees so it is a case of applying to further and higher education colleges if you wish to get a qualification and grounding in basic skills. There is no set route to becoming a journalist: you can enter the profession as a teenager or much later in life and from any background. Some of the journalists interviewed for this book had begun their training in vocational media courses at further education colleges before starting work with a media company; others had gone on to further study at higher education colleges running Higher National Diploma (HND) and degree courses. The important thing is that you do what you feel happy doing and do not try to push yourself too far in the mistaken belief that successful journalists must have credentials and lots of letters after their names. Some do, but many don't.

Do I need to go to college to become a journalist?

This frequently asked question is based on the idea that some talented individuals can still walk into jobs as broadcast journalists and feature writers without ever having had a lesson in journalism. Which is rather like believing the myth that some people can pass a driving test without ever taking a driving lesson. Whilst it is true that some people can still get jobs in journalism without holding a qualification, generally most candidates for journalism posts need a qualification recognized by the media industry. And, although it might be said that a good journalist doesn't need a degree, a capable journalist must be comprehensively trained in order to function in a highly technical workplace.

For broadcast journalism, you need a Broadcast Journalism Training Council (BJTC) qualification. A National Council for the Training of Journalists (NCTJ) qualification is needed for print.

Courses are normally run by lecturers who have had considerable experience as broadcasters and journalists, which means that the student receives professional expertise, guidance and feedback throughout their course of study. Lecturers know what is required of professional journalists and will therefore structure course exercises to emulate working conditions. They also have many contacts in the industry who can help when you are seeking that first job.

Both the BBC and ITN run training schemes for postgraduate applicants. However, these courses can only take a limited number of applicants and are liable to be changed depending on policy at the time. For primary training purposes, it is cost efficient for broadcasters to take students who have already paid to do courses at accredited colleges where there is access to state-of-the-art equipment. After such a course, the student is ready for employment.

There was a time, not so long ago, when it was not necessary to do a media course, and there is a generation of people working in the media today who entered the profession without qualifications. Some had come from theatrical backgrounds and possessed good voices and communication skills, whilst others had worked in telecommunications or electronics and had the right technical skills. Television camera operators often had a background in photography.

The various roles they filled were salaried staff positions where there were frequent opportunities to transfer to different departments and accumulate skills through daily work practices. Somebody who started their career working on light entertainment programmes could find themselves being promoted to other areas of broadcasting such as sports broadcasts, children's programmes or documentary units. There was plenty of opportunity to move around.

Today, there are far fewer staff jobs, and less opportunity to move around the various departments. People are recruited for the skills in which they have trained, and so if you have trained in journalism, then a journalist you will be. And you will be expected to have the prerequisite skills in place before starting work.

Choosing the appropriate course

The whole purpose of the course you choose is to make you into a journalist. This is achieved through training, intellectual development, analysis and research. It is not the piece of paper you hold and frame at the end of the course that matters to your prospective employer; it is the fact that the course you completed and graduated from was accredited by a national body such as the BJTC for broadcast, or the NCTJ for print, journalism in the UK.

There will be more information about BJTC and NCTJ approved courses later in the chapter.

Further education courses

There are various media courses on offer to applicants just leaving school and 'mature' applicants over 19 years old. It is not easy to decide whether to do a one-year full-time course or a two-year part-time course. It helps to plan ahead as much as you can and to try to estimate where you might be in two, three or even five years' time. Do you want to work for the local paper? National magazines? BBC News and Current Affairs? If you draw up a rough plan of where you want to be and what you want to achieve, the easier it is to choose a course of education.

If you want to work for the local paper, then a media course at a college of further education may be enough to get you started and provide you with the basic skills that will get your career under way. The first thing to do is to talk to someone at your local newspaper who can give you advice; then talk to the media course leader at your nearest further education college.

Applicants aged between 16 and 19 years, who have been successful at 'A' level study, can proceed to higher-level studies at either college or university. The idea behind vocational courses is that they allow you to apply your learning abilities to an occupational area. There are GNVQ (General National Vocational Qualification – SNVQ in Scotland) Advanced and BTEC National

Diplomas, both of which provide a route towards employment or higher education.

Vocational courses place emphasis on the successful completion of assignments set within a programme of work and study. The work is hard and the student is expected to accept responsibility for the completion of all assignments, some of which will be independent study. Assessment tests are a regular feature of the course. Set out below are just some of the GNVQ media courses currently available:

- GNVQ Intermediate Media (duration 1 year)
- GNVQ Advanced Media (double or single award; 2 years)
- Advanced Level Media Studies ('AS' (Advanced Subsidiary) level; 1 year)
- Advanced Level Media Studies ('A' level; 2 years)

Entry requirements vary depending on whether you are applying to join the course straight from school, or whether you left school years ago and are now returning to education as a mature student. Details can be obtained from the college. Generally, media courses comprise modules or units made up of core skills such as: video and radio production; photography; research and design skills; desktop publishing; writing; analysis, and so on. Much of the work is practical in nature.

Tuition fees might vary depending on where you live, your age and personal circumstances. Ask the college to which you are applying about concessionary fees, as you may be eligible. And don't forget to budget for the materials you have to buy such as books. Sometimes, former students will sell their textbooks, so it is worth asking the course leader about this.

If you fancy working for some of the larger national media companies, you might consider a higher education course such as an HND or degree (in any subject) followed by a postgraduate diploma in broadcasting or journalism.

Higher National Diploma

HND media courses are full-time and take two years to complete. Some courses can be taken at a further education college with the award validated by a university, so if moving too far from home is a problem, this may be an answer. Candidates applying from school should ideally have four GCSEs at grade C or above. GNVQs are also considered on an individual basis. Mature students without these qualifications are normally considered on individual experience and achievement.

If you intend to work in journalism, make sure that the course is relevant to the work you intend eventually to apply for. For example, it may not help to take a course in the moving image if you want to work solely in print or radio. Make sure the course fits your requirements.

Undergraduate courses

Undergraduate media courses in journalism studies, broadcast studies, media communications, media production, public relations (PR) and media or design and media, are academic and incorporate a largely theoretical approach to the changing world of media and journalism. This is not to say that there are no practical elements within each course, because there are. However, 'occasional' practice is not enough to guarantee employment after graduation.

Undergraduate students study a multifarious range of media-related interests and disciplines that prepare a solid foundation for postgraduate training or further academic study. These include: photography, writing as a craft, multimedia authoring, desktop publishing, design and advertising, video shooting and editing, radio production and presentation, and the investigation of specialist areas such as film, or literary studies and cultural studies.

Cultural studies make up the foundation of media study in higher education. This means getting to grips with the academic side of your chosen vocation. However adept you are in teeline shorthand or using a tape recorder, you will still need to get to grips with academic theories relating to media and visual culture.

Before you can become a correspondent, you must attend the lectures and read the books relating to cultural studies. These elements of the course make for a significant percentage of your eventual grade and can make a big difference between a third or lower second class honours degree and a high first. When applying for top jobs, the best employers are not interested in applicants with low degrees.

The academic approach to journalism and media studies provides the student with an opportunity to study not only the history of newsgathering and production, but also the autobiographical experiences of the newsgatherers themselves. You learn that there is no such thing as a single perspective on 'truth'; that journalism can be used for propaganda under certain social conditions; and the signs and signifiers that make up a photographic image.

During the second year of the course, you will have the chance to take part in work placement with a media company or institution of your choosing – provided that is, your chosen company can include you in its busy work schedule for a few weeks. Work placements are open to students as young as 15 years in some circumstances. See 'BBC Work Experience' at the end of this chapter for more information.

Work placement provides an ideal opportunity in which to establish contacts with the real media world. Some students get their first job through having taken part in work experience. It is the primary function of work experience, or 'case study' as it is known, to observe the media at work and write a dissertation on the experience. It doesn't mean that you will be assigned a job by the editor or be paid for what you do; but you might be given the chance to shadow a reporter during your placement.

For your final year you will have to write three dissertations: two minors of approximately six thousand words each, and a major of ten thousand words, which must incorporate cultural analysis. It is no good simply writing journalistic pieces as if you were writing for the *Guardian*. The examiners are looking for well-crafted academic papers, not feature articles.

Teaching staff often have experience of professional practice within such areas as print journalism, broadcasting, public relations, the film industry, desktop publishing, design and website authoring. There are also opportunities to meet visiting professionals working in the field of media and who spend some of their time as associate lecturers teaching undergraduates. Other guests from the world of media may also visit to talk and answer questions about their careers.

Students on undergraduate courses can and do enter their chosen media professions directly after graduating, though it is often necessary to do further vocational training to gain an accredited qualification.

Typical entry requirements: 18 points at 'A' level. Mature applicants without formal qualifications should demonstrate relevant experience and interests in related subjects.

Qualification: BA (Honours) degree. Successful completion of a degree course results in a Bachelor of Arts Honours degree. However, should the candidate fail to gain the minimum amount of points required, but completes the course, they will be awarded a BA degree without honours.

Postgraduate courses

Print/broadcast

Postgraduate courses are practical and vocational and made up largely of exercises which simulate the real world of news reporting. Students learn how to interview people, work in a team, write and produce bulletins. As daily practice, these exercises soon become second nature with constant feedback and appraisal until such time as the student is doing it right. In addition to practice, there is also the theory of journalism to be learnt: sources of information, what can and can't be said or printed.

Law makes up a considerable part of journalism courses. The Freedom of Information Bill will soon become law in the UK, and journalists will have to be familiar with it. For example, if you have to interview the victim of a sex attack, you have to know what constitutes the Sexual Offences Act, and not just parts of it.

Public administration also forms part of the course structure. This is important, as journalists frequently have to contact regional councils. County councils, district councils and parish councils, all have distinct roles to play in community politics and the journalist has to be familiar with all of them. These are just some of the minimum recommendations set by the BJTC and NCTJ. (Colleges accredited by the BJTC and NCTJ are frequently reviewed in order to maintain their accreditation.)

Online Journalism

As 'technoculture' is still being explored and expanded, global definitions as yet lack uniformity. Students of online journalism are very much part of this history-making process and so the pages, as they stand, remain to be written. This is a particularly interesting development in new media global communications, especially as the Internet migrates from the PC to more personal items such as the mobile phone, wristwatch and spectacles.

Applicants should possess good writing and computer skills, plus an ability to design. Students will design and maintain their own websites, take part in work placements, submit a written study and generally demonstrate their critical knowledge of censorship, access, copyright, legislation and much else.

Typical entry requirements: for either course, a first degree in any subject or relative experience, or demonstrated interest in a relevant industry.

Qualification: Postgraduate diploma (PG Dip.).

Finding work as a journalism student

When you attend open days and interviews in the run-up to choosing a college, ask your prospective course leader what the opportunities are for finding part-time work with local media companies. Most colleges are based within reasonable distance of a media company and often forge close links.

If you find a place, bear in mind that this should not be voluntary work. You need to make money to help with your living expenses. It would be unfair and unethical for an editor or manager to expect you to work for nothing but experience. Earning money for your work also fosters a professional attitude in you.

If there are no jobs available, then be enterprising. Write short pieces for the local paper as a correspondent. There isn't much money in this, but it gets you known. If you are good at photography, put together a portfolio and approach newspapers and magazines. Many professional press photographers have started their careers this way. (More about press photography in Chapter 12.)

If you are confident of your writing ability, try writing features for magazines and newspaper supplements. Some top feature writers started this way, and some articles (fillers) need not be very long – just a couple of hundred words on an interesting or amusing topic. You could also record packages for your local radio station – though you will be expected to supply material recorded on broadcast-quality equipment and to have edited the piece to time. (More about freelance journalism in Chapter 7.)

If you are doing a postgraduate course, there will normally be links between your college and a local media company where weekend, plus early and late shift rosters, need filling. Your course leader will foster these and encourage you to participate; all you need do is put in the hours. It is no fun getting up at the crack of dawn to drive 20 miles to the local radio station, but a good journalist is always on call.

Learning at home – correspondence courses

Correspondence courses can offer a great deal and provide you with a press card at the end of your study. However, if this is the route you wish to take, be careful. Courses can be expensive with no accreditation at the end. Also, you have no fellow students with whom to compare notes, or one-to-one contact with tutors. This is particularly important because you need to be making contacts if you wish to get on in journalism.

The National Union of Journalists (NUJ) approves just a few correspondence courses, so check first to see whether the course being offered to you has NUJ approval. Alternatively, write to the

Association of British Correspondence Colleges (ABCC),
PO Box 17926
London SW19 3WB
Tel: 020 8544 9559
Fax: 020 8540 7657
E-mail: abcc@msn.com
Internet: www.homestudy.org.uk
Also:

Open and Distance Learning Quality Council
16 Park Crescent
London W1H 4AH
Tel: 020 7612 7090
Fax: 020 7612 7092
E-mail: odlqc@dial.pipex.com
Internet: http://www.odlqc.org.uk/odlqc

BBC work experience

The BBC receives over 40,000 enquiries each year from students
wishing to gain work placements as part of their coursework. Some
departments attract more interest than they can cope with, while
many others are undersubscribed. The BBC is trying to distribute
the bulk of these applications across the four directorates –
Production, Resources, Broadcast and Worldwide – each of which
has various departments.

If you are interested in applying for work experience at the BBC in
London or in the provinces, ask for an information pack from:

Work Experience Placements
Outreach Unit
BBC Recruitment Services
PO Box 27118
London W12 8ZL.
Tel: 020 8225 9883
E-mail: work.experience@bbc.co.uk

For the contact book

Universities and Colleges Admissions Service (UCAS)
Rosehill
New Barn Lane
Cheltenham
Gloucestershire GL52 3LZ
Internet: http://www.ucas.com

2 | INTERVIEW WITH ADRIAN BUTTERWORTH

Adrian Butterworth, 27, did a degree course in broadcast studies at Falmouth College of Art, UK. After graduation, he worked for an independent local radio station in Somerset before returning to Falmouth to study for a postgraduate diploma in broadcast journalism.

Q   *Why do you want to become a broadcast journalist?*

AB When I did the degree, I saw the broadcast journalists running about, and I was very impressed by it. I just thought it would be a nice thing to do. I like the glory of it, I suppose – to a certain extent. The glamour of presenting the news, having your name on it and everything else. Instead of doing a job where nobody knows what you're doing, as a journalist they can listen in and hear the final product.

Q   *How do you perceive that glamour? In the way broadcast journalists appear on television? Or in the way they sound on radio?*

AB In actual fact, it's not a very glamorous job at all. To the perceptions of 'outside' people, it is. Once I got into it, the major thing that interested me was talking to people.

Q   *What is the average age of students on the PG Dip. Broadcast Journalism course?*

AB About 23, 24, but there are different ages. I'm the third oldest. There's a chap who's in his late thirties, me at 27 then everyone else is between 21 and 27. So it's fairly young – this year anyway. I know they've had older people in the past.

Q   *Why is the postgrad PG Dip. Broadcast Journalism course so important to your career?*

AB Basically, I'd been working as a news editor. The thing with doing that was, I didn't understand the law. So when you're ringing up the police and, say, you have a situation where somebody's committed suicide, and the police say they've found drugs in the room. Now, do you report the fact that there were drugs in the room? Do you, when you're rushed and pushed, accidently construe that the drugs were used in the suicide or were the cause of death? Without knowing the law, without knowing the background of what you can report, you can get yourself into deep trouble very quickly. If you work for the BBC, you're going to be expected to do court reporting. I also had no idea of the construction of local government stories and it's such a minefield; it's very difficult for someone to explain to you in five minutes. I could have gone away and read books and learnt it myself, but it would have been hard work.

Q   *How valuable in terms of career advancement or academic advancement, was the BA Honours Broadcast Studies course?*

AB As far as technical skills are concerned, the BA course helped in that I had done digital editing on a computer, did a small amount of presenting, a small idea of what was going on. I don't think that's the main value of a course like that; it's designed to be an academic course; it gives you an appreciation of the way the media works in contemporary society which means you can either exploit that, or at least use it in the way you broadcast. If you go into a radio station, you can look at the type of broadcasting, the audience grouping, you can analyse it in a structured way – which you've gained from the degree. So I think it's definitely helped me; not in the ways people think. Everybody assumes that because I did a degree in broadcasting, that means that I have some amazing vocational experience in producing news. Which of course I don't. The course educates you; it improves your mind, so that when you come to do a vocational thing, you can analyse it from a distance.

Q   *Could you have achieved much of your ambition simply by doing that course alone and supplementing it with on-the-job training?*

AB   I managed to start working as a news editor basically by at least leaving out some information. When I walked into the station on the first day, they said, 'What have you done in the past?' I said I did broadcasting at Falmouth College of Art, knowing full well that they'd assume I did broadcast journalism – which they did. They said, 'Right, on Thursday you can be the duty newsperson that day and we'll see how you go.' I thought, 'Oh my god! I have no idea what I'm doing.' Turned up Thursday morning; a couple of hours later, everyone went off and left me in the building on my own to get the five o'clock news done. I'd never interviewed anyone, never done a phone interview. I'd had a quick tuition on how to use the editing system the night before, but … I was very lucky. I managed to get all the interviews [done] and edited before five o'clock. The only problem with the whole broadcast was that I 'sang' it; I didn't have any presenting skills at the time. The pitch was all over the place, but the sound levels were fine. I'm now very attuned to listening to sound and making sure it's at the right level.

Q   *Do you have a career plan?*

AB   No. Not in the slightest. I have an open mind to whatever's going to happen next.

Q   *How do you think prospective employers will view your qualifications once you've graduated from this course?*

AB   I would have thought that I look eminently employable with good experience in the industry, plus a postgraduate in broadcast journalism. I would expect to be treated very well. Of course, until you've had a year working for a BBC station or whatever, there's still slight doubt there, but this course has a 99 per cent employment record.

Q   *What can you learn on this course that you couldn't learn elsewhere?*

AB   Nothing really, but it's all in one place. In an intensive year, all organized for you, all you have to do is put in the hard work. To try and achieve the amount of learning you can do in a year here, while you're working, would take you many years just sitting down and reading the books and trying to work things out on your own. It's a fast-track way of getting a big body of knowledge about the industry very, very quickly. And, of course, work with industry professionals.

Q *What about the cost of doing a course such as this one?*

AB Now, that's a problem, yes. I came out of the degree owing to the bank and the student loan company. This course costs £3,500 in tuition fees alone, and you've got to add maintenance to that, so I took the full career development loan and there's interest on that.

Q *How is the course affecting your personal confidence? Do you feel more like a professional or professional-to-be, than you did on your BA course?*

AB Oh yes, absolutely. But I have had experience as a news editor now. I have actually been a boss running my own newsroom. It's going to be an interesting question for those that have come from a degree course. I'm sure it's a big surprise to them walking in here because you've got to treat it as a job. It's at least nine to five, and you've got to have some maturity in the way you time-manage. But yes, to me, it's a totally different situation. Number one, I wear sensible clothes to college now. And, at the end of the day, there's no point in arguing what you're taught on the course; it's not open for discussion; it's the way the world is constructed; the way journalism is.

Q *What sorts of subject are you covering on an average day doing the PG Dip.?*

AB I get up about half-past seven, watch the TV news for an hour or so; look at teletext, the local and national papers. Then in for nine-thirty for the news meeting where they ask us to give them 40 seconds on a local story and then they'll come back at you with questions as if you were questioning a reporter from the studio. The average day would consist of journalism skills – being taught how to write cues and news stories – or broadcasting skills – making programmes, magazine programmes, doing the news, researching stories; basically what you'd do in a newsroom. Other days, there would be law and public admin., politics. We've had lectures on health and safety, leadership skills ...

Q   *What about work experience?*

AB   Next term, we've all got a weekend with a local radio station. And then in May we've got a month's work experience. Most people are going to be in radio – local or independent.

Q   *Is there anything you'd like to add?*

AB   People think that to be a good broadcast journalist or to do well in the media, all you have to be is ruthlessly ambitious. I've seen many people use this route and they upset everybody. Nobody likes them; they don't like other people. They tend to take it all too seriously. They don't think, and eventually it causes them more problems than they could ever have realized. You've got to be able to handle stress and not be too ambitious. Being a presenter on television may sound impressive, but it's equally as valid to be a presenter anywhere else. They should relax and it will all happen for them anyway.

Q   *Thank you.*

3 | JOURNALISM IS ...

One definition of journalism is that it gives people the essential elements of an event without making it simplistic. And if, as a journalist, you can achieve that, then you achieve journalism.

(John Pilger talking to John Dunn, BBC Radio 2)

Regardless of whether you intend to work in print, Internet or broadcast journalism, the methods used for obtaining news will be much the same: sourcing, interviewing, writing-up, presentation/reporting. The tools differ, but the processes for newsgathering and reporting are much the same across all media.

Some journalists are as adept at doing a piece to camera as they are at writing column inches for a broadsheet; whilst others prefer to remain in just one medium. Don't worry that you will be asked to work in all media – you won't. That choice is always yours.

The following chapters examine the roles of the press reporter, radio journalist, TV news reporter, photojournalist, freelance and specialist journalist. Aspiring journalists should read all these chapters, whatever their specific career goal, as basic journalistic practices and techniques are common to all media.

The role of the press reporter

From the very first day you start work in a newspaper office, the pattern of work will not change dramatically throughout the rest of your career regardless of the medium you work in.

Finding your way around

When you start work, some of the older hands may regale you with stories of when they first started for the newspaper – running messages and fetching coffee – long before they got their first assignments as 'cub reporters'. It may sound whimsical nostalgia for a bygone age, but it was often a good way of getting to know the newspaper, the offices, the people and the way everything functioned. Today, new employees can often find themselves in at the deep end, trying to operate highly technical equipment and dragging their new colleagues away from important tasks just to find out on which shelf *Who's Who* is kept.

So before you start work, ask the editor if you can spend a day familiarizing yourself with the layout and contents of the newsroom and the offices in general. This will mean spending a few unpaid hours getting to know your way around, but it is worth it because it is important that in order to check facts, as you will have to do from day one, that you know where to locate information, and quickly. A large amount of your work will be based in the newsroom, so get to know where the reference books are, their titles and what subjects they cover. Once you start work, no one will thank you for continually having to drop work in order to direct you to whatever you need. You will also need to know where to find and how to reference archive material, newspaper cuttings and files stored on CD-Rom or the computer network's hard drive. In time, most archives will be stored as electronic data, but for the immediate future, a mixture of archival systems will exist in many offices.

Familiarize yourself with the telephone and fax systems and photocopier. Obtain a telephone list of staff names and their extension numbers, and make sure that you know how to reroute a call. Getting to know your colleagues is another important part of the job: after all, you will need to get to know the community the paper covers, so start with your colleagues.

Contacts

From day one, you will need to begin listing contacts. The paper will probably keep its own contacts book or equivalent in a software file – to which you will be expected to contribute by placing the names, numbers and addresses of useful people you meet in the course of your work. You should also keep two books of contacts for personal use. These contacts are invaluable, so whatever you do, keep a second log of identical entries in a different place and do not discard any information just because you move on. It even pays to keep further records on a floppy disc and the hard drive of your PC.

Day one

Depending on the policy of the paper you work for, either the news editor or chief reporter will brief you on your first assignment of the day or you will find assignments logged in a diary. You may be working alone or with another reporter for the first assignment, but your training will have prepared you, making it an exciting experience, not a frightening one.

Whatever the nature of the assignment, you will need to check facts, which is why that all-important familiarization of the office is so necessary. You might have to refer to newspaper cuttings from the archive, check some files on the C drive or CD-Rom, make telephone calls, or a combination of all of these before you set foot out of the building. Indeed, many assignments require office-based resourcing and interviewing where you won't need to leave your desk. This saves time and money for the newspaper, but is less fun for the reporter.

However, where possible, it is important from day one to make contacts by going out and getting to know who's who in the local communities that the paper covers. When you meet councillors, police officers, health workers, farmers and many others, make a point of introducing yourself and get to know something about them and the work they do. Some papers supply their reporters with personal calling cards that include the paper's title, address and the name of the reporter. Hand these out and make use of them; make your own if you have to.

You may find that through covering local politics your interest in national politics grows, and before you know it, you are on the way to specialization. Certainly the skills you learn at this early juncture will be useful throughout your entire career.

Interviewing

Interviewing people is not a simple process, and getting it right is one of the most difficult parts of journalism.

For a newspaper, you may be interviewing everybody and anybody, from schoolchildren to visiting celebrities. Don't be put off by some people's brusque manner; provided you go about the business of interviewing in a fair, straightforward and professional manner, you will have nothing to worry about.

Before interviewing someone in person, try to find out something about them through research. For example, if you are interviewing the town's chief fire officer, archival material in the form of press cuttings may give you an idea of their background, such as number of years in the fire service or awards given for bravery.

Most interviews can be recorded using a notepad and pencil, but if you anticipate there might be a future legal challenge regarding content or if the interview is likely to be lengthy, use a tape recorder or mini-disc.

Jot down some preliminary questions, and consider the objective of the interview. What is it you want to find out? Do you want just to talk in general and note what is of interest, or do you have a particular question that you would like answered? Whatever it is, make a note of it and underline it: 'I want to know why ...' Use the preliminary questions as stepping-stones to get you to the objective.

Once you are conducting the interview, be prepared to let the conversation flow. You may find out much more than you bargained for. However, do not let the interviewee divert the conversation away from the things you want to ask. Stick to your objective.

Do not ask the interviewee things they cannot be expected to answer: Fire chiefs will talk about topics related to their work – nothing else. Do not put words into their mouth. And if the interviewee says, 'This is off the record, but …', then however exciting the information, off the record means just that: you cannot use it. Be ethical at all times as good ethical practices always serve the journalist well.

There are exceptions to off-the-record: public meetings are always *on* the record, so if in a public address, someone says: 'My statement is off the record', it is not. When anyone agrees to talk to you, it is considered that the information they pass on is on the record unless they state otherwise.

Always be prepared to listen during the course of the interview and be sympathetic where sympathy is required. It is not your job to act as inquisitor, so do not push a question, especially when the interviewee is distressed.

Telephone interviews

In respect of UK and international laws regarding tape recorded interviews conducted over the telephone, you should tell the interviewee that you intend to record the conversation.

At the beginning of the call, give your name, the paper you represent and the person you wish to speak to. Be sure of the subject you want to talk about and be specific. Check spelling on names and titles; over the phone the letter *S* can sound like *F*, and *V* like *B*.

'Applebury Divisional Fire Station. How can I help you?'

'Hello. My name is Jane Smith, I'm from the *Advertiser*. Can I speak to the chief fire officer, please? It's a press enquiry into the reduction of staffing levels.'

Telephone searches

If you are trying to locate people through directory enquiries, bear in mind that the operator has access to the same information as you do: a comprehensive listing of numbers published in the telephone directories. Most newspaper offices stock the entire collection of national telephone directories and Yellow Pages. The only difference is that the operator can call up the information quickly on a computer screen.

Operators will not give out addresses, although they will confirm an address. Don't waste time pleading for ex-directory numbers; operators cannot give ex-directory numbers because they do not have access to them. Ex-directory means just that.

Internet searches

Newspaper libraries can supply the journalist with material in the form of original press cuttings and from electronic databases. Both types have advantages depending on the story being covered. No one wants to be snowed under with boxes of cuttings when researching a big story.

In addition to the paper's library, the nationals have their own libraries, some with archive material dating back to the beginning of the twentieth century. Check with your editor before calling a national newspaper's library as there may be a substantial cost involved.

On the Internet, you can use search engines to trace names of individuals and companies. Parliamentary Commons debates can be followed at http://www.parliament.uk; and CD-Roms are useful sources of information: *UK on CD* lists the electoral roll, for example.

Notebooks

A journalist's notebook is kept as an accurate record of journalistic notes taken for a report. It acts in a similar way to that of the police officer's notebook, meaning that notes can be used as evidence in a court of law. In this respect, it must be used meticulously, with dates, titles and names accurately entered. It should not contain frivolous notes such as shopping lists or doodles; nor should it have pages missing from an entry.

When entering information, fill out each page in full – leave no blank spaces where somebody else could add material if they had access to it. Title each story, date it and include your name and the name of the subject(s) you interview. When you have completed a notebook, file it; do not discard it.

Staying out of trouble

Staying out of trouble is not easy as a reporter. However, providing you are honest at all times and face your editor with the truth as you understand it, life will be bearable. Do not attempt to make excuses or hide the truth.

If, when covering a court case, someone tries to bribe you, reject what is offered and turn away. Never keep money that has been thrust into your pocket. Inform your editor immediately and confirm it in writing with a memo.

When dealing with verbal complaints, do not blame someone else or argue back. Listen carefully to the complaint being made, however rudely, making notes of the complainant's argument. Take down their name, address, the phone number and details of the article to which they are referring (date, edition, page number). Then inform the editor or deputy editor. Never try to deal with the complainant alone, and do not admit liability or blame anyone else. Politely and calmly inform the complainant that you have taken note of what they have had to say and will inform the editor immediately.

Reading other publications

When not writing their own material, reporters need to read other people's. Start with your own paper, keeping abreast of its daily or weekly contents. Read what the competition is producing as well as regionals and nationals. If you are working for a weekly, the story you are working on could have appeared in another publication earlier in the week. Through reading the earlier publication, you can update the story by calling your contacts for developments. You must, however, make reference to the original story.

Familiarize yourself with the magazine market, especially those that are produced locally and cover the same ground as your paper. Listen to local and national radio stations, tuning in to different programmes at different times so that you have a comprehensive knowledge of what is being broadcast. Watch the TV for local and national news broadcasts and programmes of interest. And without leaving your desk, make it a daily routine to surf the Internet. Bookmark sites of interest. Try not to become selective and habitual in what you consume – taste it all.

The benefit of all this consumption of various media is that you start to build up your own cuttings file and greatly increase your local and national knowledge of news and current affairs. Understandably, it would be too expensive to buy various publications each week, but you can visit newspapers on the Internet (a list of recommended sites is given below). Make a point of visiting libraries – especially university libraries if there is one near – and ask friends and neighbours to unload their unwanted periodicals on you.

Surfing the Net

For national and international papers online, try:
http://emedia1.mediainfo.com/emedia
http://ajr.newslink.org/news.html
http://www.discover.co.uk/NET/NEWS/news.html

You can take a look at Parliament by hitting:
http://www.coi.gov.uk/coi

Talking of ethics, try:
http://www.uta.fi/ethicnet/ethicnet.html

Before calling directory enquiries, try:
http://www.switchboard.com

Books

B. Hennessy and F.W. Hodgson, *Journalism Workbook*. Focal Press, 1995
Contents include: helpful advice on early assignments for journalists at the beginning of their career.

F. W. Hodgson, *Modern Newspaper Practice* (4th edition). Focal Press, 1996
Contents include: finding the news; layout and design; running a newspaper; and much more.

Richard Keeble, *The Newspapers Handbook* (2nd edition). Routledge, 1998
Contents include: learning the language of news; covering the courts; feature writing; and much more.

4 | INTERVIEW WITH TRISTAN NICHOLS

Tristan Nichols, 22, is a trainee reporter with the *Evening Herald*, Plymouth, UK. He went to Plymouth College of Further Education for two years and attained a GNVQ from a media course. He passed his course with 31 distinctions, 9 merits and a pass. He was also Student of the Year and has since been invited back to give talks at the college. At 16 he was working on his village parish magazine and has worked hard to attain his current position.

Q   *How did you learn of a job vacancy on the* Evening Herald*?*

TN   Sheer fluke. I went on work experience to the *Evening Herald* from school and college. I went into various different departments – graphics department, classified and finally ended up on the newsdesk. It was through these connections at the *Evening Herald* that I eventually got in there.

      I'd been taken on at the *Sunday Independent* (a regional paper covering the west country) two weeks after I left college.

Q   *That was your first job?*

TN   It was my first job in the industry. I left college, and signed on. I was enrolled on the New Deal government scheme (to help place people in jobs) and I got a call from their office telling me about a placement at the *Sunday Independent*. So I wrote off and went for an interview. I was taken on for a six-month trial as a trainee reporter and after that period was over, I was invited to continue. I stayed for 18 months working in their Special Publications group, producing trade papers and learning about everything, but I had no experience of reporting.

Q *How did you make the transition from trade papers to reporting for a newspaper?*

TN I was working alongside journalists from the *Sunday Independent* on a daily basis, and I expressed an interest in writing stories for them. I started submitting material about friends of mine taking part in different events. And that's how I got in on the *Independent* ... Although I spent only a couple of months there, working voluntary.

Q *You weren't being paid?*

TN No. I was only being paid to work on special publications. After working for the *Indy* for a couple of months, I received a phone call asking me to attend a meeting the next day saying that Special Publications were being moved to Falmouth. I wasn't prepared to move down there as I'd just purchased a flat, so I started to write and ring around. That's when I rang the *Herald* and they called me for an informal chat and suggested I put a letter together and get an interview with the editor. I managed to do that, got the job, and I've been there four months now as a trainee reporter.

Q *Will you be going on an NCTJ course to become fully qualified?*

TN There are plans to send me on a course once I've spent some time with the paper.

Q *Can you tell me what you remember about your first day as a reporter?*

TN I've never really been good on the phone. I remember getting grilled by my news editor because she wanted me to ring this guy at half-past eight in the morning. I got his number and rang him at work only to be told he wasn't in yet. So I put down the phone, but my boss said, 'That's not good enough, you must speak to him. Can't you get him at home?' And I'm thinking, 'I can't ring him at home, it's half eight in the morning!'

Q   *Did you initially have problems in finding your way around?*

TN Not really, it's just a case of asking people how things work.

Q   *People were helpful in that respect?*

TN They were. As long as you show enthusiasm, people are willing to offer a helping hand. You've also got to go out and learn as many technologies and techniques as you can. It all benefits.

Q   *Can you tell me something about your daily tasks?*

TN I always listen to the radio first thing in the morning to get the news on Plymouth Sound radio. I also watch the news on the television, then read through teletext, go into work listening to Plymouth Sound updates on the car radio. In work, I pick up the *Western Morning News*. I sit at my desk and have a look through PA [the Press Agency: a computer-generated database that provides stories on a local and national basis and comes straight through to each reporter's terminal], see if anything's come up there. I have a look at the diary for the day.

Q   *What exactly is the diary?*

TN It's got everyone's name listed and any number of things that you've got to do today and tomorrow. It's so important to keep track. If you say to someone, 'I'll call you next Tuesday,' you've got to make a note of it. And the work diary is the facility that you use. It's a case of looking at the diary, speaking to the news editor to see what's going on, cracking on with anything that's happened nationally overnight that has any local angle.

Q   *Are there times when there's nothing to do?*

TN No, no. There's always something I can generate if nothing's happening. I can ring contacts. I'm covering Pete Goss's story a lot at the moment. Anything I find interesting, I follow up.

Q   *Do you keep your own contact book?*

TN   Yes I do. I've actually got three.

Q   *To whom are you directly responsible at the paper?*

TN   We've got four news editors.

Q   *What shifts do you work?*

TN   Any number of shifts. There's 6.50 am to 3.30 pm; 8 am to 4.30 pm; 10 am to 6 pm. Then there's the late shift, which is 2 pm to 10.30 or 11 pm depending on what's going on. At weekends, you've got shifts starting at 6 am, 7 am, 8 am and, I think, 10 am. That's just a few hours on the Saturday, and then on the Sunday you have one person who comes in at 8 am, I think, and the next at 2 pm, just to put the calls in on stand-by.

Q   *Do you find it easy to relax when you're off duty?*

TN   I don't really switch off. When I get home I put on the TV – not to watch *Neighbours* – but to watch the news. Pick up the paper and read the paper while I have tea. If I go for a pint, people always ask me what's going on at the minute and a big discussion gets under way, so you're never really off duty.

Q   *When you've finished writing up a report on screen, do you deliver it to the copy-desk as hard copy or do you upload it in a file?*

TN   If I interview someone over the phone, I note down the details into my notebook, then write it up on screen then upload it through the computer system.

Q   *I understand you recently covered the story of Pete Goss's sea trials in which the catamaran lost part of a hull?*

TN   I got a tip-off from a friend of mine who works for the *Mirror* telling me that Pete Goss was sinking off the Isles of Scilly. I didn't believe him at first, but I rang up the news editor and told him. Initially, he didn't believe me and I had to convince him. He told me to call him back in five minutes, which I did. He told me to catch a plane from Plymouth

Airport saying that he'd see me again on Friday morning. This was Wednesday morning, so I spent three days in this quaint little island of St Mary's, where I'd never been before, with about 35 journalists from the world's media. I didn't even have a toothbrush or a change of clothes, or anything at all. I used to be a scout where the motto was be prepared; I was obviously forgetting that.

Q *How did you keep in contact with your paper?*

TN I rang up the news editor and told him what was going on. He wanted 350 words and put me across to the copy-takers. I was standing there on the edge of a pier, freezing cold, with a pen and a notepad and I had to look out to sea, see this catamaran and explain how I was feeling. It wasn't a case of getting just facts, the story was happening right there, so I had to explain on the spot the tragic situation that these people were in. A £4.5 million super-yacht nearly sinking.

Q *Did you get to speak to the skipper, Pete Goss?*

TN I managed to stow away on a BBC boat and we sailed out and cruised around the catamaran a couple of times. It was quite an experience. That Wednesday night, we all went out for drinks. I was up by 5.30 in the morning, feeling rather rough, standing on the edge of the pier when Pete Goss came in and I managed to grab a few words with him before anyone else arrived. He also held an informal press conference.

Q *How did you file your copy from the Scillies?*

TN I phoned up the news editor who put me across to the copy-takers and I talked it down the phone.

Q *When you're writing reports in the newsroom, what type of computer are you using?*

TN It's a Mac with a Word Windows package.

Q *Can you touch-type?*

TN No, but I can type pretty fast. I don't have to look at the keyboard all the time.

Q   *Do you use shorthand?*

TN I'm just learning it. I started learning about two years ago but didn't follow it through.

Q   *Do you take pictures to accompany reports?*

TN Sometimes for vox pops [a collage of brief interviews with members of the public]. I'm not a trained photographer, but I do go out and take vox pops if I need to get a quick comment. It's nice to publish a 'face' to accompany it.

Q   *Are you expected to be able to use a camera?*

TN It's kind of expected.

Q   *Are you supplied with a camera and film?*

TN Yes, a point-and-shoot [compact] camera and film.

Q   *How do you see your career developing?*

TN I want to do everything. I sometimes feel there aren't enough hours in the day for the things I want to do. I want to go into different forms of media, try my hand at television and radio. I absolutely adore what I'm doing at the moment.

Q   *Do you get fed up of working in your hometown?*

TN No, not yet. There's still a lot that I'm learning about Plymouth, and I was born here. Once I feel I've really got a grasp of it, I'll progress from there. I want to work 'national' one day.

Q   *How many hours a week do you work?*

TN Around 40. That's for the paper, but I come home and I attend meetings and whatever, go to functions, so I'm still working then. People fascinate me. Everyone's so different, each person has a different role in life, so I always go out and do my best to meet them.

Q   *What holiday entitlement do you get?*

TN I think it's five weeks. Three years ago, I'd have had a heart attack to hear that you could work 40 hours a week and get only five weeks holiday a year, but it was just a case of easing my way into it through college and work experience. And then it becomes, 'Who needs a holiday? I want to work!'

Q *How much of your work is done from your desk in the newsroom?*

TN I'd say about 80 per cent.

Q *Isn't that frustrating?*

TN It's all that I'm used to, so it doesn't frustrate me that much. People on the other end of the phone get annoyed because I can't come out and meet them. I like having the security of being in the office.

Q *Are you expected to perform other roles in the newsroom, such as subediting?*

TN Yes, we are now. They've just brought in a new computer system called TERA. Basically, it allows the reporter to write a page with catchlines, straps and headlines, and construct their own bylines. It also allows the reporter to sub. It's a great system; it's really worked out well as it allows the reporter to get so much more involved in their work. Rather than just bashing out a story and seeing it the next day, you can actually bash out a story now with the headline and strap and everything, and look at it the next day and think, 'This page was mine! I designed it.' Everyone's really taken to it.

Q *Does your paper incorporate the Press Complaint Commission Codes of Practice?*

TN Yes, it does. When I first joined there were plenty of notes on the desk saying what to do, what not to do. One of the news editors talked me through it all and someone came down to give me a day's lecture on it.

Q *Do the codes impede your work as a journalist?*

TN Not really. Not on a local level.

Q   *Do you feel that as an individual journalist, you can influence the editorial content of your newspaper?*

TN   It's up to you as a reporter to bring a story forward. The reporter 'sells' the story to the news editor. You've got to make the most out of any given opportunity; get the best angle out of a story and then inform the news editor that that's the direction you want to take with the page. I don't report on the harsher sides of life anyway, at the moment. I'm dealing with the lighter side of life. I'm still learning.

Q   *Are you a member of a trade union?*

TN   Yes, I'm a member of the NUJ.

Q   *Is there anything you'd like to add?*

TN   Only that I got here through sheer enthusiasm and really going for broke. I just smile a lot; I'm a cheery person. I didn't send death threats to the editor or anything like that!

Q   *Thank you.*

5 | WRITING

Writing has prehistoric roots that can be traced to early tokens being placed in clay and then marked to show what was inside and what goods were promised as payment – two bushels of wheat or whatever – signified by a personal mark in the clay. These early 'cheques' promising to deliver, bore the marks of the bearer – not just a thumbprint, but a recognizable symbol: the first character and also the first signature. It wasn't much, but it was a beginning.

Good copy

'Get me copy, fast!' can be an oft-heard demand from many a copy editor's desk. It is not an unreasonable demand when a daily paper needs to fill blank spaces urgently. What the copy editor does not shout, however, is 'Get me *good* copy, fast!' It is taken for granted that what should fill the paper's blank spaces is, indeed, good copy.

What is good copy? Good copy is well researched, well written, concise, informative, pertinent, attention-grabbing and, most importantly, edited.

The days when writers would leave subeditors to the hassles of cleaning-up rough prose are over. It is not enough to be creative with ideas; you must be able to spell and use grammar correctly. The role of the subeditor has changed, and in some cases, disappeared altogether. Nor is it enough to place faith in the computer's grammar/spell-check, as there are some things that the computer just cannot recognize as being a mistake.

A news writer does not have to be a budding Graham Greene, but literary skill is, nonetheless, important. In order to bring life to the text the writer must have an aptitude for the work. Even the most sedate of news reports requires cadence and rhythm if it is to be printed.

Study the papers

If you are employed to write for a newspaper or magazine then you have to write in that publication's style. This isn't as easy as it may at first appear. You will need a good eye for style if you are to adapt to writing it. Study as many papers as you can and note what defines their style. Not all broadsheets are the same, and not all tabloids are the same; it takes time and effort, but it is a worthwhile exercise.

Now choose a topical news item of which you have some knowledge and which is currently being run in several newspapers. Write a report in a style which you think is close to that of each of the newspapers you have selected. For this exercise, getting the facts right is not as important as getting the style right.

When you've completed the exercise, check for similarities. Does your *Guardian* piece run to a similar length to the real one? Would your piece for the *Sun* appeal to a *Sun* reader? In your piece for *The Times*, have you used similar key words and phrases? If so, what are those words? *The Times*, for example, uses a wide vocabulary and sophisticated construction, whereas items in the *Sun* are short and punchy. This does not mean that shorter items are easier to write. Sometimes it can be more difficult getting the main points of the story across in 100 words than in 350.

What is style?

Literary style refers to a distinctive way of writing that can be defined by the reader as well as the writer in much the same way as an accent or style of speech. For example, the use of staccato sentences or lengthy descriptive verse; specific terms, buzzwords or jargon, can all signify an individual author's style. The use of a unique literary style is fine for the novelist, but the news writer is expected to drop any pretensions to an individual style in favour of that of the publication – its house style. House style refers to conventions regarding sentence and paragraph structure and length; the use of titles, names and numbers; punctuation, abbreviation and capitalization. House style has been created by publications especially to harmonize production, reduce confusion, make the text easier to understand and to establish an identity in the reader's mind. By observing house style, the textual content of the publication remains consistent over time even though the news content and writers change on a regular basis. Consistency in language is the sign of a good publication and a skilled team of writers.

Style, whether it be your own or that of the publication, should be a by-product of the effort to communicate clearly on paper rather than something that is consciously created. Trying to write in a particular style can detract from the objective of writing news. The primary objective should always be to use an ordered method of providing facts through clear and concise writing.

House styles should be in the background because the reader is interested in facts, not whether the writer has prize-winning potential as an essayist. The content of the piece should never affect the overall style.

Far from being restrictive, house style saves time by preventing writers and editors from making countless decisions about how to spell a word, abbreviation or number. The guidelines are clearly established and easy to follow in a stylebook. House style also helps in preventing conflicts between writers working as a partnership or team. One writer does not have to modify their work to conform to the individual style of the other.

To summarize:

- Stylebooks harmonize the production of copy for writers, editors and publishers.
- Text is easier to read and understand when spelling and punctuation is consistent.
- Stylebooks clarify the use of figures: 3 pm as opposed to 3.00 pm or three o'clock; £10 replaces £10.00 or ten pounds.
- Stylebooks provide a guide to the use of punctuation, spelling and grammar.

The only time that style favours the longer version is if there is a possibility for confusion: this usually applies to technical terms, abbreviations and acronyms.

In the case of some tabloids, shortened versions of words act as signifiers for the paper's unique style.

Vocabulary

Like the editor, the writer should always include among personal resources a dictionary, thesaurus and synonym finder. If referred to often enough, these books will not only solve day-to-day problems, but also help to improve a writer's ability as a wordsmith. And developing a curiosity about words is a good way to build vocabulary.

As a matter of course, always look up the meaning of words or terms you cannot define. Common sense and the dictionary should be your guide. Making a list of new words or phrases will also expand vocabulary.

Webster's is the dictionary for American-English usage, and a must for all writers who need to refer on occasion to American variations in spelling. It also lists British-English equivalents but should never be used as an only source when writing British-English. For British-English usage, the *Oxford English Dictionary* or *Chamber's* is recommended.

A thesaurus not only lists more impressive or learned synonyms, but it can also be used to find alternatives to multisyllabic words or buzzwords.

Editing your work

Editing is as much about attitude as practice. It is all too easy for a writer to admire their creation so much that it becomes difficult to cut words and phrases that seemingly add pace and animate the piece. To adopt the attitude of editor and stand aside from the work in order that extraneous material can be pruned, is a task that requires much self-discipline.

Theoretically, the process of editing should not be difficult. After all, the writer's aim is the same as that of the editor: to produce good copy that has clarity and brevity. And the most effective way for a writer to do this, and to adapt it to a publication's house style, is to read the copy carefully and to make changes. Before being handed to a copy editor, all copy should be edited by the writer to clarify content, correct grammar and eliminate trite phrases.

Editing can enhance an otherwise dull piece. It must be said, though, that careful revision and editing is not a luxury most writers can afford when working to a deadline. In the past, there has been a natural adversarial relationship between writers, who do not like to have their copy cut, and editors. This is not surprising, as editors constantly malign, and rightly so, the use of metaphors, redundant phrases, clichés, unclear abbreviations and buzzwords which collectively inflate the language but add little meaning.

Graduate journalists are frequently the worst offenders when it comes to inflating the language. Inflation is learned at schools and colleges when essays are padded with extraneous material in order to reach the required minimum wordage. It is during this primary stage of the student writer's development that they place great emphasis on the length and sound of words rather than on their meaning. This pressure can result in clear communication being lost.

Most writing can be tightened up. Spotting and deleting words and phrases, without losing the essential meaning, is the essence of skilful editing. But how does the writer avoid platitude when under pressure?

Inflation

In journalism, where space may be at a premium, if one word can be used in place of many, then there is more room for facts. Synonyms avoid monotony, but you should not replace simple words with multisyllabic words or with phrases. Use a short word in preference to a long one. Use a short word *instead of* a long one.

Generally, keep sentences short. Try to aim for sentences of 30 words maximum. Longer sentences, when used in conjunction with those of ten words or less, can add variety to the piece.

Introductions and paragraphs

Whether writing news or features, the introduction (intro) is the most important part of the article – especially the first few words, which must not only catch the eye, but also contain the primary elements of the story as concisely as possible. From the intro, paragraphs (pars) break up the body of the text into digestible pieces for the reader. The purpose of a paragraph is to contain a sentence or sentences that describe a theme within the subject of the article. Each paragraph propels the narrative to its closure, like scenes in a play.

Paragraphs must link smoothly. This is where adverbs can be put to good use: *as*, *inevitably*, *indeed*, *however*, *meanwhile*, *nonetheless*; all make good bridges, as do conjunctions such as: *and*, *but*, *when*, *if* and *that*. In some publications, a paragraph might be only one sentence.

Don't be afraid to use paragraphs and, as with sentences, vary their length.

Adjectives

Use adjectives to describe or inform – in moderation.

Be specific

Trying to keep articles clear and concise is one thing, but exact information is what is required of the news writer. Exact information tells the story accurately and paints a comprehensive picture in the mind of the reader. Pack sentences with facts and particulars: the objective being to supply specific information.

Don't be vague:

Example 1

A large lorry lost control and embedded itself into the wall of an old cottage near Wolverhampton. Witnesses to the crash say the lorry was travelling at speed when it lost control and ran off the road into the cottage. Engineers say it will be difficult to remove the lorry without the wall of the cottage collapsing. The driver and some bystanders were taken to hospital suffering from shock.

(69 words, 362 characters, 5 lines)

Be specific:

Example 2

In a desperate bid to avoid a pedestrian, a ten-ton articulated lorry ran off the road and embedded itself into the wall of a seventeenth-century cottage. The lorry, carrying frozen meat, had left its Wolverhampton depot just after 8 am – 30 minutes before the accident happened on the busy A454 in the village of Trescott, yesterday. Witnesses say the lorry was travelling above the 30 mph speed limit when the driver lost control and ran into the cottage. Structural engineers say supports and heavy lifting gear are required before the lorry can be removed from the damaged front wall. The driver and two bystanders were taken to hospital in Wolverhampton suffering from shock. Nobody was in the cottage at the time of the accident.

(126 words, 613 characters, 9 lines)

The first example would suggest that although vague, the article is not inflated with extraneous words. The second example carries details about the accident but is almost twice as long. Can it be reduced without losing the detail?

Example 3

In a bid to **avoid** a **pedestrian**, a **ten-ton** lorry left the **busy A454** before crashing into a **seventeenth-century** cottage. The lorry, **carrying meat**, left **Wolverhampton** just after **8 am – 30 minutes before** the crash in the **village of Trescott, yesterday**. Witnesses say the lorry was travelling **over the 30 mph limit** when the driver lost control. **Structural experts** say **supports and lifting gear** are needed to remove the lorry from the **front** wall. The driver and **two** bystanders were taken to **Wolverhampton** hospital suffering from shock. **Nobody was in the cottage at the time of the crash**.

(99 words, 483 characters, 7 lines)

Although not as short as the first article, this edited version is shorter by 27 words, 130 characters and 2 lines, whilst retaining all the specific points. Where possible, longer words are replaced with shorter ones: crash replaces accident; experts replaces engineers.

Clichés

Avoid clichés like the plague. Sorry, it was difficult to resist, and therein lies the problem for writers. Clichés are irresistible because they're convenient and easy to find. Journalists have little right to condemn the clichéd phrase as it is often the newspaper writer who creates them in the first place.

It is not the first few uses of the cliché that cause consternation, but rather continual use until it loses its appeal. In a world dominated by global communications, clichés soon become overused and tired.

When editing, seek out the cliché and substitute with direct terms. Use clichés only in the context of quoting dialogue, as most are spoken, not written.

Example 1

After his spectacular crash, former champion rally driver, John Smith said: 'That part of the course was so dark, I literally couldn't see the wood for the trees.'

Example 2

Union negotiator, Bill Jones, said that he was 'confident both union and management would hammer out an agreement.'

However, arguments can be made for the use of some clichés within a certain context where the writer feels the cliché is apt and cannot be replaced.

Jargon

For writers in the special-interest and trade press, the jargon of technical language will be understood and even expected by readers. In general news and feature writing, avoid it, or, if it has to be used, explain its meaning.

Abbreviations

As with the use of jargon, writers should not assume that readers will be familiar with all abbreviations. Write definitions in full immediately after first using the abbreviation and do not introduce another abbreviation for the same term without first explaining it.

Not all abbreviations require explanation. RAF requires no explanation, nor do RAC and AA. Used in context, some well-known abbreviations do not require explanation although the two latter examples would be accompanied with the description *motoring organisation* to differentiate them from the Royal Armoured Corps and Alcoholics Anonymous:

> *A regular pub visitor, Mr Smith was rescued by the AA on many occasions. A spokesman for the motoring organization said: 'We're always pleased to help our members.'*

Another way is to spell out a name or term the first time it is used and follow it immediately with the abbreviation in parenthesis:

> *The bank has been inundated with complaints about its new automated teller machine (ATM).*

Facts and events

The journalistic rule of explaining an abbreviation the first time it is used should also apply to mention of any facts and events that the reader might not know or have forgotten. For example, the term Glastonbury is commonly used in print to describe the annual pop festival held in Somerset. It should not be confused with the town of Glastonbury, which is some miles away from the event, so information regarding the festival can be introduced like this:

> *The organizers of the Glastonbury pop festival held annually near the village of Pilton, Somerset, hope to break attendance records this year ... Attendances at Glastonbury have been down in recent years.*

Or:

The high-profile break-in was likened to Watergate, where, in 1972, government documents were stolen on the orders of high-ranking government officials. The subsequent inquiry brought dismissal from office for presidential aides, H R Haldeman and John D Ehrlichman, and most dramatically, the impeachment of President Richard Milhous Nixon.

Redundancies

The problem with the English language is that there is such a large vocabulary to choose from; it is tempting to use too many words. Hence redundancy. In a bid to reduce clichés, do not make the mistake of incorporating redundancies.

Example 1

The council's decision to build environmentally friendly houses has been welcomed by conservation groups. Green in colour, the houses will jointly share common land set aside for growing fresh vegetables. At the advance planning stage, councillors welcomed the opinions of eco experts, and said they would welcome their proposals in future planning. That all the houses have now been completely finished ahead of time has come as an unexpected surprise for the council, although the actual facts behind the purchase of the land have still to be revealed.

Edit out the redundancies, and the article reads thus:

Example 2

The council's decision to build environmentally friendly houses has been welcomed by conservation groups. Painted green, the houses will share land set aside for growing vegetables. At the planning stage, councillors welcomed the opinions of eco experts, and any proposals. That all the houses have been finished ahead of time has come as a surprise for the council, although the facts behind the purchase of the land are still to be revealed.

Here are some more redundancies:

After numerous meetings, and much verbal discussion, the council successfully passed the plans for the eco development.

Redundancies are difficult to spot until the writer trains the eye to recognize them at a glance. Look for duplicate meanings and cut to the essential. Thus:

After meetings and discussion, the council passed the plans for the eco development.

The following are examples of commonly used redundancies:

totally dead
follow later
fed up of
different to
nearly perfectly
more recently
filled up

Mixed metaphors

Metaphors can be used to good effect in creative writing. Used correctly, they can evoke the most descriptive of images in the mind of the reader; but avoid overuse. In news writing, the frequent use of metaphors can, like the cliché, suggest the writer is searching for any convenient phrase to fill space or to complete a sentence. Head for any port in a storm by all means, but stay within the context of the piece and use sparingly.

Unless the writer's aim is for comic effect, mixing metaphors is the best way of demonstrating an ignorance of both metaphors and clichés, as the following jumbled phrases demonstrate:

■ You can take a gift horse to water but you can't make it drink.

■ The pilot fought with the controls to get the plane back on track.

■ We were up to our necks and time was of the essence.

Euphemisms

Euphemisms need not be avoided because they allow the writer to convey meaning without having to resort to inappropriate terms. The subjects of war, sex and death rely on euphemisms where graphic and unambiguous descriptions cannot be used in deference to public taste and sensitivities. War reporters refer to *casualties*, *collateral damage*, *smart bombs*, *friendly fire*, *deny with extreme prejudice*. These carefully crafted phrases are usually issued by the public relations offices of military defence departments whose job it is to present war in supposedly palatable terms in order to minimize public outrage or panic.

Reporting of sex scandals or crimes often incorporates terms such as *sexual favours*, *compromising position*.

Euphemisms surrounding death have frequently been coined by undertakers, doctors, police and armed forces to lessen the impact of bad news: *deceased*, *laid to rest*, *mortally wounded*, *didn't regain consciousness*.

Buzzwords

Buzzword, meaning an invented word or phrase that sounds important, is in itself a buzzword. However, just because they sound important, doesn't mean they are. Buzzwords often begin life in advertising, politics and other promotions. Picked up for everyday use, they are placed randomly in text as a way to impress and promote the latest fad or ideology. Computer language has brought a whole host of buzzwords to the language: *Internet*, *download*, *user-friendly*, as has academe: *hegemony*, *generic* and *Zeitgeist*, all of which are gaining in popularity through some publications and broadcast programmes.

Capitalization

A general rule is to capitalize proper nouns only.

Nouns as verbs

One of the changes in journalistic styles in recent years has been that of creating verbs from nouns. Apply caution, however, and avoid using nouns as verbs when writing news. 'The President is to helicopter to Camp David tomorrow afternoon' will probably cause a groan from an overworked copy-taster.

Names

Double-check the spelling of names because there can be various ways to spell personal names.

Times, dates, figures and currency amounts should also be double-checked.

Edit *how* many times?

Before handing over copy to the copy-desk, review the facts line by line with a ruler, paying particular attention to names, titles and figures. Then read it again checking for general spelling, grammar and punctuation. Ask yourself whether it flows, and do not be embarrassed to read it aloud – your colleagues probably do the same with their copy. If you are reasonably happy with it, take a short break before reading it one more time.

6 | WRITING NEWS

Shorthand

Like touch-typing, shorthand is a skill that, once you possess it, you'll wonder how you did without it. For an NCTJ National Certificate or GNVQ, the trainee journalist must be able to write at a minimum speed of 100 words per minute to pass the exam. Shorthand is an excellent form of taking notes at speed, especially in situations where you cannot use a tape recorder or mini-disc (council meetings, courts) and situations in the field where there is no power and no replacement batteries to be had.

Even for those journalists not intending to take a qualification and work on a newspaper, shorthand is always useful. Many further education colleges advertise shorthand courses that can be taken at evening classes or through drop-in sessions. Do bear in mind that it is much easier to learn with a tutor than trying to learn purely from books and tapes. Also, it is not possible for a complete beginner to achieve the required speed of 100 words per minute by the end of an accredited journalism course, which is normally 12 weeks; so start learning well in advance of joining a course. Of the two systems used, Teeline is most commonly taught and used. Pitman was once the only system taught to aspiring secretaries and journalists.

When reporting, be sure to carry several pens and pencils at all times. HB pencils are particularly good for shorthand.

Keyboard skills

Learning to touch-type will be another great advantage. Once you have learned you will be able to type at speed without having to look at the keyboard, which is ideal for when you have to transcribe notes.

There are some excellent computer software learning programs available so that you can learn in your own time, or you can attend courses at colleges and adult education centres. As with shorthand, allow yourself plenty of time to get up to speed.

Writing skills

There are several genres of news writing: hard news, soft news, news feature; colour feature and backgrounder. All of these genres share components such as description, background, quotations and analysis, but hard news is specifically the reporting of new information relevant to the reader. The term should not be associated purely with the reporting of wars, crime, disasters and national politics; it can include news of golden weddings and what's happening at the athletic's club.

Although writing news differs from writing fiction, it is equally as reliant on the introduction for grabbing the reader's attention. Depending on the length of piece, the news writer must convey these important points in the opening paragraphs of the story:

- Who
- What
- Where
- When

Often, all of these points can be included in the opening paragraph:

Gangland leader Freddie 'Fists' Fumpel [who] was arrested [what] at his home in Effney Green [where] last night [when].

These are the same questions that you would use if investigating a story: Who is involved? What happened? Where did it happen? When did it happen?

With such a methodical approach to gathering news, writing it becomes so much easier. You've already done the groundwork; all you have to do is write it in a narrative order that makes sense to the reader who may be coming to the story fresh or with some knowledge of the event.

The intro should not attempt to provide all the main points of the story. For example, *How* and *Why* can form the middle part of the story:

> *Police, acting on a tip-off, made the arrest following the shooting of Fumpel's arch-rival, Billy 'Bugs' Bugnall, in an Effney nightclub two days ago.*

Would this story work with a slightly different arrangement?

> *An arrest was made at the home of gangland leader Freddie 'Fists' Fumpel in Effney Green, last night.*

or:

> *Freddie 'Fists' Fumpel, the notorious gangland leader, was arrested at his home in Effney Green, last night.*

The sentences still contain the essential points of who, what, where and when, but in different word order, they fail to catch the attention in the same way as the opening word 'Gangland' in the first example.

Word order is important. As soon as the reader spots the word 'Gangland', they know this introduces a crime story. This is backed up by the opening word of the second sentence: 'Police'. These are words that are crucial to the angle (main theme) of the piece and help to give the subeditor a headline for the story. It has only to be scanned by the eye to reveal its subject matter. This is no ordinary arrest of a minor offender. This is big time.

Because papers contain so much information, and the reader's time might be limited, it's easier for the eye to scan words and pictures than to try to read each story in full. Few people read every column inch of a daily newspaper so it is important for the writer to capture the attention with carefully worded comment. Use verbs and nouns to make an impact.

What about the rest of the story?

Example 1

It is believed Fumpel (52) had gone to ground after Bugnall (46) was rushed to hospital on Monday night to have two bullets removed from his chest. Two days after the shooting, Bugnall's condition is said to be non-life-threatening.

The gangsters – rivals for control of Effney Green's four gaming parlours – were once close associates, both having served time in Openville Prison during the 1970s for armed robbery, fraud and deception.

After the arrest, a police spokesperson said they had acted on 'sound information' and were confident that Fumpel could be linked to the shooting.

Remember that if the subeditor is going to cast off (edit the story to fit) they'll remove the last paragraph; this is normally considered the least important as writers put essential information at the head and middle of the piece leaving the tail to be sacrificed if needs be.

The same story construction applies to the report of a wedding anniversary.

Example 2

A couple who met in an Oxfordshire pub at the height of the Second World War, celebrate their 60th wedding anniversary this week.

Alfred and Rachel Modelip were both serving King and country in 1943 when their paths crossed in the bar of the Red Cow, Weston-in-the-Wood – then a frequent watering-hole for young service personnel stationed nearby.

Had it not been for Rachel walking into the bar and ordering a glass of water, Alfred, a trainee navigator, might never have approached her: 'I was also drinking water, and thought it was refreshing that someone else was likeminded. I just had to say hello. And I thought she was very attractive in her army uniform.'

The couple married in 1946 and set up home in Moatley where Alfred worked as a clerk for the town council. In 1961, they moved to Cutswell with their three children, Mark, Alan and Debbie.

To celebrate their anniversary this Sunday, Alfred and Rachel will reaffirm their vows at the parish church of St Anne's, Cutswell. After the service, the couple, along with family and friends, will drive 30 miles to the Red Cow pub at Weston-in-the-Wood for a celebratory meal and drinks – water is optional.

Both of the above examples are linked by the human angle: 'gangland leader' and 'couple' are terms that lead into the piece. People make the news so it makes sense to lead with them.

Propelling the narrative

Just as the fiction writer propels the narrative using a traditional method of storytelling – hero/heroine meets agent of change – problem (disruption) – hero/heroine's quest – return to normality (closure) – so the news writer propels the narrative of the factual story by placing events in sequence. Unlike the fiction writer, the news writer cannot create the events that form the narrative, but it is necessary to present them in a manner that makes sense to the reader.

Imagine that you are reporting a fire that is believed to be the result of arson. You have quotes from both the chief police officer and the chief fire officer. Both are relevant, but which do you use first as part of the intro?

This is the quote from the chief police officer:

Example 1

'This is the third suspected arson case in as many months. There doesn't appear to be one particular motive, but we're linking this to the other two fires because of the petrol can and burnt rags found at the rear of the building. We are particularly interested in talking to the owner of a green van that was seen in the vicinity just before the fire started.'

And this is the quote from the chief fire officer:

Example 2

'We are currently searching the building for other evidence, but I can tell you that we have found a burnt petrol can and rags at the rear of the building which would indicate the fire was started deliberately by someone placing rags soaked in petrol into the door frame and setting them alight. However, we cannot rule out the possibility that the fire was started in more than one place which is why a thorough search is being made at this moment.'

Firstly, count up the number of points of news interest in the quotes.

Chief police officer:

- Suspects arson based on evidence
- Cannot find a motive
- Linking evidence
- Looking for a vehicle
    = 4 points

Chief fire officer:

- Co-ordinating search of building
- Has found evidence
- Believes fire may have been started in more than one place
    = 3 points

Remember, too, that arson is a criminal offence, meaning that a police officer will take charge of the investigation. If the fire were accidental, it would be the fire officer responsible for the investigation into the causes.

Now you can start putting down notes:

> *Police suspect arson as a third industrial building is razed to the ground in recent months. Whilst firefighters continue to search the rubble for further evidence, police want to talk to*

the driver of a green van seen in the vicinity shortly before the fire started.

Although a burnt petrol can and rags have been found at the rear of the building, the chief fire officer is not ruling out the possibility of the fire having been started in more than one place.

As yet, police are unable to find a motive behind the fire but are linking it with two previous fires based on the evidence of the petrol can and rags found at the rear of the building.

In this preliminary draft, you've used up the points you made, but you still need to put things in order of priority. You've mentioned the burnt petrol can and rags twice, so one can be cut. The use of 'Although' to begin a sentence softens the impact, so cut that sentence. Start paragraph 2 with the chief police officer; paragraph 3 with the chief fire officer. Fill out the piece with background: time fire started; the owners/tenants of the building; any products made or stored there; whether dangerous or not; future plans for production. Sum up with details of other relevant information: McKeefer's and the other two fires.

1 *Police suspect arson as another industrial building – this time on the Wellingford Park Estate – is razed to the ground. This is Wellingford's third serious industrial fire in recent months. The building, which is owned by Landfalle Estates but rented to McKeefer's Plastics, caught fire just after 9 pm Tuesday night and has been completely gutted. A spokesperson for McKeefer's Plastics is 'bewildered' as to why they should be targeted.*

2 *Whilst firefighters continue to search the rubble for further evidence, police want to talk to the driver of a green van seen in the vicinity shortly before the fire started. Chief Police Officer Ranauld Mathari told our reporter: 'There doesn't appear to be one particular motive, but we're linking this to the other two fires because of the petrol can and burnt rags found at the rear of the building.'*

3 *Wellingford's chief fire officer, Kim La Pelle, is co-ordinating a detailed search for further evidence behind the cause of the fire and has not ruled out the possibility that it may have been started in more than one place. Ms La Pelle assured our reporter that no toxic gases were released during the fire.*

4 *McKeefer's Plastics produces plastic pipes and guttering for industry and began trading from the site in 1992. It employs a workforce of 120, most of whom work full-time in production. A company spokesperson said that although the premises were fitted with fire alarms and sprinklers, and had recently been inspected by the fire safety officer, no security cameras were fitted.*

5 *Fires at two other industrial sites on the outskirts of Wellingford in June and July resulted in the combined loss of 500 jobs plus an estimated £5m in lost production for local companies Arendales and Treddar's.*

Let's see if this narrative structure has worked.

Paragraph 1

This begins with urgent phrases ('Police suspect arson – razed to the ground') and contains the first bit of background information on the building's owners and tenants. In essence, the first paragraph should be a summary of the story. Although quotes and partial quotes are acceptable in the opening paragraph, the last sentence, 'A spokesperson for McKeefer's Plastics ...' doesn't fit well here; especially when there is another reference to McKeefer's and partial quotation from the spokesperson in paragraph.4. Remove it and place with the later reference; this will also help the last sentence to flow into the next paragraph linking 'gutted' with 'rubble'. Within the reference, the word 'bewildered' has been included as a partial quote and highlighted with inverted commas and attributed to an unnamed spokesperson to convey the feeling of loss. Use partial quotes sparingly as they can be confusing when used throughout the story. Note the time written as '9 pm' – not 21.00 or 9.00 pm. This is the most concise form and the most commonly used in newspapers.

Paragraph 2

Paragraph 2 should continue the flow of information and expand on the intro by including background information such as the firefighters continuing to search for evidence. The direct quote from the chief police officer expands the angle. The quote is used in full (which the subeditor may cut) but there is no explanation regarding evidence at the other fires, leaving the reader to assume that petrol cans and rags were also found at the rear of each building. This suggests the arsonist was leaving deliberate clues. Never leave the reader to assume – be specific. If the arsonist is leaving clues, it will make a good follow-up. Note the inclusion of the rank 'chief police officer'; it is important for the writer to show what authority the comment has come from and also demonstrates that the authorities are taking the fire seriously. The inclusion of titles in full can be problematic; in this case, the police chief can later be referred to as Mr Mathari.

Paragraph 3

Starting the sentence with 'Wellingford's' places the origin of the chief fire officer, which is particularly important for a local paper. Readers want to know that their emergency services can cope when necessary. If they cannot cope, then there is another good follow-up story. As with paragraph 2, the focus on the chief fire officer places the report in the present tense: the fire has been extinguished, the gutted remains are now being examined under her guidance. Until the next publication, this is how things stand with the story. It would be wrong to reveal in the next paragraph that there was a further development.

Paragraph 4

This paragraph examines the background and human cost of the fire. Note the convention of reporting McKeefer's as 'produce[s] plastic pipes' – not 'produced' in the past tense. In reality, no more pipes or guttering can be produced from this site. This refers to the fact that the company was in production up to the time of the fire. Nor is there mention of the exact number of job losses – only the number (120) that make up the workforce. At the time of going to press, it is not known whether the 120 will be out of work. They may be re-employed at another site for the same company. Because the company spokesperson is saying very little and does not want their name to be published, little is known about the fate of the workforce. However, mention should be made as to whether anybody was working or present in the factory at the time the fire broke out.

Things to watch out for

- Opening lines with a quote: 'I intend to resign,' says council leader Mrs Nardine Neswa. These openings are rarely used because they rarely work, especially when the subject is not well known.
- Avoid opening with a figure unless it is the main point of the story: Two hundred and fifty workers are expected to lose their jobs ...
- Don't open with a number: 250 workers are expected to lose their jobs ...
- Don't open with a question: Will you still be visiting your high street bank in five years' time?
- Better: Online banking could threaten the existence of high street banks if new proposals ...
- Don't delay the main point: The man who scored more goals than any other, Danny Fabshaw ... Better: Danny Fabshaw, the man who scored more goals than any other, ...
- Leave the oblique opening (delayed drop) to the feature writer: When people visit the bank tomorrow ...

Books

Nicholas Bagnall, *Newspaper Language*. Focal Press, 1993

The catchline should head each folio (page) and give in order surname of writer, publication title, the editor responsible for the section you're aiming at, and a single word to identify your piece followed by the folio

Pridmore : Daily Advertiser : Attn: Jane Smith : ROAD 1 of 5

For those who love to meander down the little roads of England, the A39 has much to offer, especially if you want to leave the car at home.

Don't use common catchlines such as 'Fire', 'Accident' or 'Poll'. Also, leave space for the sub to write a headline

With a desire to meander, I determined to travel and off rural, short-haul buses as they plied westward My goal – to reach journey's end in Falmouth in whatever time it took.

Ideally, copy should be wordprocessed or typed, double-spaced with wide margins top, bottom, right and left. This follows a traditional format

The A39 is the only 'A' category trunk road to be Porlock Hill it becomes the steepest 'A' road, and at Lynmouth, the most narrow. To say that it twists, turns, curves and gently meanders, is to seriously understate the fact.

Speeding the modern family touring car along this highway in an effort to reach a resort quickly, is not advisable. The frequent, tight curves just don't allow for it, nor do the frequent tractor-towing-trailer excursions. And that's not what this road is about though, sadly, developments for wider and straighter lengths are under way in certain places.

If, like me, you fancy taking the slow road as a passenger on a succession of buses, you'll start off across the Mendips, traverse the Quantocks and Exmoor, and keep the sea within sight for most of the trip down. I should catch and when.

...MORE

Don't run on from one sheet to the next in the middle of a par. Use a fresh sheet of paper if necessary

Just as the catchline heads every folio, so the word 'More' should follow at the foot of each folio with the exception of the last. This tells the editor that more pages are to follow – a great help if they get scattered across the desk or floor. 'MF' is a term used in news stories and means More Follows. At the foot of the last folio, type 'ENDS' or 'END'.

Figure 7.1 How to lay out copy on the page

7 FREELANCE PRINT JOURNALISM

It is a myth that in order to work as a freelance journalist you must have had a career as a staff journalist. Some of the world's most successful freelances have never had a lesson in journalism. Nor is it necessary to have ability in shorthand or qualifications in law or photography. The freelance is a writer who can ply their trade using nothing more than a wordprocessor and a telephone.

Throughout the 1980s and 1990s, newspapers and magazines began to make large cutbacks in their permanent staff, which was ironic considering that editions were getting bigger with new weekly and weekend supplements. The number of new magazines being launched was also at an all-time high. Of the many cuts being made, editorial departments took their share.

This large-scale redundancy was countered by the proliferation of freelance copy being sent 'on spec', with both newspapers and magazines receiving unsolicited copy daily. Not surprisingly perhaps, this coincided with the growth in ownership of wordprocessors and personal computers'. This burgeoning expansion in user-friendly writing aids and the demand for more and more print was providing a goldrush for entrepreneurial freelances who grasped the opportunity when they saw it. Many were unknowns who had never worked in a newsroom but were sure they could supply something the papers would be interested in.

Critics might also say that this was a period in which hard news was being replaced with features of little consequence. Under new ownership and new directives, both newspapers and magazines steered their publications away from the wars and starving towards homespun 'lifestyle' material: 'The gardens of the rich and famous' or 'How to convert your loft into a study', are just two of the many topics that have appeared regularly since the 1980s and are often written by freelances. Reviews of theatre, restaurants and cinema also provide staple fare for the jobbing writer, as does travel-writing. While the staff-writer is stuck in an office, the freelance is at liberty to go out and find their own material. Quirky stories are much in demand from both national and regional publications, and the worldwide market should also be considered.

Where to begin?

Probably the best place to start a freelance career is with regional newspapers and magazines in order to gain experience and build confidence. Whatever you do, study your target market carefully: a piece about Canadian lumberjacks, however well written, is not necessarily going to appeal to a magazine aimed at members of the Women's Institute. There are exceptions, but generally the mistake that many aspiring freelances make is to target the wrong publication. This isn't just a concern with subject matter; style, too, plays a big part in getting work accepted. Magazines, like newspapers, have a style that the freelance needs to recognize and adhere to and is not something that should be left to the subeditors to correct. When you research a publication, make a note of the style. Is the language old-fashioned and romantic with descriptive prose? Or is it hip, sharp and to the point?

Make a note too about the angle of the stories being used. Just what sells a story to this particular publication? For example, you may know of an ambitious young rock band just beginning to make a name for themselves in your local area. Their story might be good if there is an angle. If there isn't one, forget it. Just because they are a rock band on their way to a successful future does not mean there is a story – not yet, anyway.

Travel-writing

To be paid to travel to far away places and write about them seems a dream come true. In fact, you do not have to travel far from your doorstep to be a travel-writer. World tourism is constantly seeking out the new and fresh – anything that has not been tried before – so you might have the opportunity to promote an unknown corner of the world that holds a few hidden gems.

If you were to write about Disneyland, Paris, the chances are high that editors will yawn upon receiving your copy and dump it on the slush pile. Disneyland is great and people love it, but it has been written to death. Write about a sleepy suburb a few miles south of Disneyland that offers beauty, tranquillity and history, and you may be on to something.

Approaching magazines

Depending on whether your target magazine is published weekly, monthly or quarterly, the time required to publish an article will vary from weeks to months. Generally, it is a good idea to plan months ahead in the same way that a magazine's editorial team would. If you want to supply a piece on Christmas shopping and sightseeing, then you are going to have to be 12 months ahead in putting the bulk of your article together. You will not be able to research and write up a piece in the Christmas season and expect to see it published in a monthly magazine before 25 December. The seasonal edition will have been planned and set out in the late summer. Indeed, for any seasonal subject, you are going to be working a year ahead, and can expect payment any time up to 16 months ahead.

The content of monthly and quarterly magazines reflects the changing seasons and it is almost impossible to find a subject that is not related to the seasons in some respect. A piece on the New York marathon needs to be published at the time of the actual race if it is to work. However, you could do something on how one athlete prepares for the race.

The best way to approach magazine editors is to write them a letter that includes a synopsis of your feature:

Example

Dear Ms Smith,

Would you be interested in the following idea for *Horses for Courses* magazine?

American entrepreneur Tommy Bridle has recently opened a cowboy-style ranch in Hampshire where novices can learn to ride genuine American quarter horses and take part in round-ups, cattle drives and trail-riding through the New Forest. Twenty-five horses have been especially imported from Tommy's former home in Colorado and are kitted out in genuine Western tack. This is the first venture of its kind in Britain and if it's successful, Tommy hopes to open a second establishment.

Tommy opened 'Range Riders' in response to a growing demand for Western-style riding in Britain. He made his name in the 1980s as a rodeo star touring the USA and Canada before becoming a Hollywood stuntman. It was while working on a film in England that he fell in love with Hampshire and decided to buy a farm that he could turn into a ranch.

In addition to giving lessons and rides for novices, he also hopes to be able to take part in competitions and shows around the country.

I will give background, technical information on stock and tack, anecdotes and general information on prices and how to get to the ranch.

I am a freelance writer who has written various articles for press and magazines. I can supply good quality 35 mm colour transparencies, if you require.

Yours sincerely,

Jon Doh

It is important that you address the letter to an editor or deputy editor by name and not simply 'Dear Sir or Madam'. You can always ring the magazine first to find out the name of the person to whom you should send an idea and how they prefer to be titled (Ms, Mr, or full name). Do not rely completely on writers' guides as the editor may have moved on since it was published. Always include a stamped addressed envelope, and, if you are writing to a publication abroad, include an international reply coupon, which is available from post offices. Do not send the manuscript until invited to do so. If you do not hear anything within the month, by all means ring and enquire. The best decisions can take time.

Writing for newspapers

You could also sell the above story to newspapers – national and regional. There are many national readers who would be interested in the subject as riding is very popular. Also, Tommy's story may be of interest to a world readership as he has taken part in rodeos and worked in films that people have probably seen.

As with magazines, it is imperative that you study the market and respective styles of your target publication. It is no good sending this to the *Mirror* if the paper has no history of ever publishing anything like it. Nor is it helpful to send it to the editor of the *Financial Times'* women's page when it is more likely to be of interest to the features editor. Check to see where similar items are being placed. Importantly, do not try to sell the same piece to various publications without informing each of where they stand with regard first, second or third rights. If you sell to the *Financial Times* first, inform any subsequent buyers of what you have already sold and to whom.

Making contact

Newspaper editors are inundated each day with unsolicited articles from writers hopeful of having their talent spotted. However, many of these articles – some of which are well written – often do not reach their target. Sometimes the subject matter and content are inappropriate for the publication. Added to this, editors do not have the time to go through all the articles, so secretaries read through what they can. Occasionally, an article may get 'spotted', but this is not the way to sell your work.

In order to sell to newspapers, you need to call the page editor to whom you need to pitch your idea and at a time when they will be able to take the call. This requires good timing, confidence and a basic understanding of how papers function. During the morning, editors go into conference to discuss what is going into the next edition. Conference is normally over by midday and the chances are that there still isn't enough copy to fill the page, so if you time your call after conference and before lunch, your idea may have a chance, especially if you call between 12.30 and 12.50 pm.

It is most important that you find out who is responsible for editing the page or section that your piece is aimed at, so ring the switchboard and ask who edits that particular page. Before making your call, summarize your proposal in as few words as possible and have it on paper in front of you when you make your call.

When talking to an editor, especially one who has never heard of you, it is vital that you describe your idea as succinctly as you can. You can use the summary as a prompt when you are put through. National newspaper feature editors are notorious for answering the phone by speaking hesitantly – as if someone were about to shoot them. They are suspicious when calls come through to their desk from people they have never heard of, and they react accordingly.

Do not be put off. The fact that you have got through to them at a free period tells them immediately that you are not a rank amateur. Your call signifies that you know, at the very least, how to approach your work, and most importantly, how to approach them.

Make sure immediately upon being put through that you are speaking to the person you intend to speak to, and then introduce yourself. You don't want to start rattling off your carefully prepared proposal only to find that you're speaking to someone doing work experience.

A call to the paper's switchboard might go something like this:

'Good morning, *Daily Planet*.'

'Good morning. Could you tell me who edits Weekend features please?'

'Vanessa Burton.'

'Put me through to Vanessa, please.'

Always check who edits a page even if you have found the editor's name listed in the *Writers' and Artists' Yearbook* or *The Writers' Handbook*. Staff change, and you can look foolish if you've got the wrong name. A good journalist will always check first.

'Hello.'

'Hello. Is that Vanessa?'

'Yes.'

'Hello Vanessa, my name's Jon Doh; I'm a freelance writer. I've got an idea for an article you might be interested in. Would you like to hear it?'

This is the awkward moment as your question allows the editor to refuse, but out of politeness it should be asked. Do not assume that you can go into a heavy sell routine just because the editor has picked up the phone. If they tell you they have not got the time, thank them for their time and say goodbye. If not, pitch your idea.

'Well ...'

'Mikey Michaeldorf is a freelance boat designer who's disabled and he's designed a very special rowing skiff that can be rowed one handed. He's going to row the entire length of the Thames. Nobody's done it before and it's going to be a record attempt. I thought it would be ideal for the *Planet*. Would you be interested?'

The summarized proposal names the subject, his occupation, the angle (he's disabled and working against a handicap, making his effort heroic), its original (no one has done it before), and it might be published in a record book (but could be read first in the *Planet*). Lastly, you have thoughtfully added a get-out clause in asking whether they'd be interested. This shows that you are confident, but not arrogant. After all, however good the idea, the *Planet* may not want it for any number of good reasons.

'Um, ... I don't know really, ...'

'Can I fax it through to you? And if you like it – great! If not ...'

'Okay, fax it through, but I'm not promising anything. And nothing over 500 words.'

'Thanks. I'll fax it to you by two at the latest.'

This is not a commission, but it is a step in the right direction. The editor has agreed to consider a piece of work from a complete stranger. And even if it is not used, you have introduced yourself and demonstrated that you can supply copy on interesting subjects.

If it is not used, you may never find out why, but there are many good reasons as to why an editor chooses not to go with a particular piece at a particular time. Remember, too, that with a newspaper, it is no good offering a story that is not due to take place for a few weeks. Daily papers and weekend supplements need copy now.

Bear in mind that this is not a commission, so do not start haggling over the phone about what it is worth. Newspapers are very good when it comes to paying their dues for copy used. All you have to do is supply it on time and in a state that requires little, if any, work to make it fit on the page.

If the editor likes your idea and agrees to take it, ask for a commissioning note stating how many words are required and when. Always make sure you get your copy in on time and that it is neat and accurate. Paying attention to these very basic points will attract an editor to your work and make it easier the next time you want to sell something.

Structure

A good article is 'made' within the opening paragraph. Take too long to introduce something, and you will lose the reader. If you are writing about mountaineering, catch the reader's attention straight away with: 'Mountains don't come any bigger than this.'

If the material in the middle seems a bit of a haze, before you commit fingers to keyboard, jot down what you intend to include, paragraph by paragraph, and where it ought to be going. If it starts to lose purpose and direction, question what it is that is not working and either leave it out or add something else.

Par 1 My reaction on seeing the mountain for the first time.

Par 2 The anticipation as I approach.

Par 3 The pain in my legs and back as the oxygen becomes thinner the higher we climb.

Par 4 I really feel close to nature and God at this point. Very spiritual.

Par 5 The summit. I can see the whole world from here. I'm in the lap of God.

On receiving copy, editors look for the 'meat' of the piece by going straight to the middle. Experience and knowledge of convention tells them that if the writer has done their job properly, it will be sharp and interesting at the midpoint and will not have tailed off. Novice writers can open a story confidently enough and hook their reader, but maintaining that interest can be difficult, especially with long articles. If the middle fails to hold the editor's attention at this crucial point, it will be 'spiked' – discarded.

Content

You will find that, as you begin to write, various aspects of the story – that at first you might not have realized were there – become apparent.You will also begin to come to a more objective decision about the subject, as if you were the reader. Have the confidence to allow the piece to take its own shape.

Language

It is a mistake to show off writing ability when constructing an article. Use self-discipline and consider what it is you are trying to say. Do not be tempted to raid the dictionary for smart terms and flowery words that are rarely used; such language can be infuriating for readers who do not appreciate your willingness to show off. If you write: 'She had pellucid blue eyes', you might cause a lot of readers to flick the page and read another article – or throw the paper down in disgust.

It is also a good idea to 'talk aloud' the article as you write so that you get a sense of the flow of words and meanings.

Closure

The end, like the beginning, can be the best part of writing an article. Unlike fictional narratives, real events do not have closure as such. If you write of an expedition to a mountain, once you have come back down, the story does not end: you can always write of your determination to go back, as the mountain will always be there; climbers will always want to conquer it. Journalist John Pilger, who covered much of the Vietnam War for the *Daily Mirror*, often returns for the latest update on how the country is coping in these post-war years.

The last paragraph should prompt the reader to think more about the subject. Closure, therefore, should not be the final word on the subject because in reality there is no such thing as the final word. If there is to be some form of closure, then it should come from the reader as much as from the writer.

Style

Much of what attracts writers to freelance journalism is the freedom to write in their own voice and to incorporate their opinion about a particular subject. This sounds great, but a subeditor may well cut to pieces your carefully crafted account of climbing a mountain, and jumble it up in such a way that you won't recognize it. You must write to the constraints of the page. Imagine the page being put together: your story, however life-changing it was for you, will probably be reduced to fit into a small space between two adverts at the bottom of page 20. This is why your writing has got to be concise. Articles need not be long. Some of the best and most informative pieces are just a few hundred words.

Getting ideas

You don't need to specialize in a particular subject: a good freelance should be adaptable. Indeed, it is a good policy to tackle things you do not know about. That way, you are more enquiring and objective in your approach as you are not bringing any preconceived ideas to your story.

If your intention is to write as and when on any given subject, there are various methods to finding interesting topics. Like a staff journalist, you will make contacts who will keep you informed of events, but you would have to know a lot of people if you were to make a regular living from freelance work in this way.

Re-working

Some experienced freelances rework published articles. This entails reading through as many magazines as you can in the hope of finding an article that will appeal to a new readership. Very often, the more obscure the magazine, the more interesting the article. Specialist magazines are a good source, and even parish newsletters have some amazing stories.

Once you find an interesting subject, you cannot and must not 'lift' the piece: that is plagiarism, which can get not only you into trouble, but also the paper that buys the article. However, there is nothing to stop you reworking the piece. Nobody holds copyright on ideas. You should, of course, do your own research to make sure that what was relevant at the time the article was originally written is still the case and that it is not legally sensitive. Once you are happy this is not the case, you can put your own angle on the piece and sell it on. The chances are that somebody else will rework it yet again after seeing your publication.

Books, local newspapers, radio, television and websites also provide some good ideas for the freelance. All sections of the media are watching one another for ideas and news, which, of course, is how news spreads in the first place.

Training opportunities

If you are interested in a career in magazine journalism, contact:

Periodicals Training Centre
Queens House
55–56 Lincoln's Inn Fields
London WC2A 3LJ
Tel: 020 7404 4168
Fax: 020 7404 4167
E-mail: training@ppa.co.uk
Internet: http://www.ppa.co.uk

Books

The style used by many of the top freelance writers in feature writing is one that is today well established but has origins in the New Journalism of the 1950s. Journalists such as Tom Wolfe and Truman Capote were just two of several writers to develop the form. What made New Journalism so special 50 years ago was that it revolutionized the feature by incorporating the fictional styles of the novelist: describing real people, places and events with a 'colour' and dimension normally inscribed in the fictional creations of a classic narrative tale.

Truman Capote, *In Cold Blood*. Penguin, 1967

Tom Wolfe, *The Kandy-Kolored Tangerine-Flake Streamline Baby*. Picador, 1981

8 | INTERVIEW WITH KATE MOSELEY

The bread-and-butter work of most freelances is not always glamorous or exciting. Many editors look for informative copy that fits the style of their publication and that their readers will appreciate. The bulk of freelance work usually covers fairly mundane issues for magazines, regional and national press.

Kate Moseley is a freelance journalist. She trained as a home economist and has worked for the Food Advisory Service developing recipes and doing food photography. She has also worked as a copywriter and public relations executive, and for various magazines including: *Home and Freezer Digest* (cookery editor), *Anchor News*, and in a freelance capacity for *Womans Weekly*, *Now*, *You Magazine*, *BBC Good Food Magazine* and various other women's magazines. She also works as a radio public relations officer and writes and produces syndicated tapes on various subjects from pancakes to engine oil plus information and company brochures.

Q *Did you want to become a journalist or was it something you drifted into?*

KM I never thought about being a journalist, as such, although when I was at college my ambition was to be a cookery editor on a national magazine, but that was because of the recipe work and food photography rather than the writing. So, I suppose you can say I have drifted into it.

Q *Did you train to become a journalist?*

KM No, not trained. When I first joined Anchor, I went on a two-day 'how to write press releases and house newspapers' -type course. I did enter my house newspaper for an award and got a certificate, but it was so long ago I can't remember the name of the company that ran the training. I also went on a two-day radio course at GWR (formerly Great Wiltshire Radio) in Bristol – about ten years ago. Went to an evening class to learn to type – but have not been trained on the computer – so I need to hone my skills!

Q *If you were an editor employing a journalist, what personal qualities, education and experience would you be looking for?*

KM Enthusiasm for life and work in general, and for food. Knowledge of where to look for more information and ability to be able to map out features on their own and work on them, but be confident enough to ask anyone for help and more information. Friendly manner on the phone, ability to work on computer. Ability to sort out relevant info and write in a logical but interesting way. Not necessarily a graduate, or have experience – just be keen.

Q *Do you find print and radio similar or contrasting in respect of journalistic methods?*

KM There are different styles of writing. When writing radio scripts, you have to bear in mind personality and the skills of the interviewer and interviewee. Questions should be written in full, answers in notes for interviewee to expand on in their own way. Remember time is tight. Come to the point quickly. Keep it simple; it's more relaxed than the written word.

Q *Don't you get tired of writing about food?*

KM It depends on whom you are writing for. It's fine when you've written a piece and you're really pleased with it and it's printed as you wrote it, but sometimes subs, or those higher up on the magazine, get in the way and your copy can be dumbed down, or the style changed completely not just once but a few times and then it comes back to you for checking and you hardly recognize it! Sometimes some good points are added, other times it can be annoying that they've taken your 'personality' out of the piece. I have more freedom on the house newspaper, including more speech, which can make it witty and fun.

Q   *What advice would you give to an aspirant freelance journalist?*

KM Keep a book of contacts up to date so you can call on people quickly to get information. Bear in mind the publication you are writing for – its readers' lifestyles and capabilities. Think the feature through before commencing; check your research and stories, especially spelling of names. Keep articles short rather than epics. Don't labour the point. Let your knowledge and enthusiasm shine through so it's an easy-going, enjoyable, inspiring piece of prose, tempting the reader to try the food/recipes.

Q   *How do you think journalism has changed since you first started?*

KM I was using an old typewriter, had to type to fit certain column widths. We [literally] cut and pasted copy – used a lot of Spray Mount, lost bits of copy in the bin! Turning copy into proofs took two to three days, returning proofs to printers took a few more days, then any copy changes after that cost 'lots of money'. We worked six months in advance and had the magazine printed in Finland.

Q   *Do you think that changes have been for the better?*

KM It's great to be able to do your copy on the computer and e-mail stuff over with pix [pictures], and design on the computer as well. I don't use the Internet a great deal yet, but I'm sure that speeds things up. The only problems are other people tweaking your copy more easily now!

Q   *Is there anything you'd like to add?*

KM Read or flick through as many other publications around your subject as you can. Keep tear-sheets of work you have enjoyed reading – and bad examples. Keep a note of brilliant headlines or feature ideas that suddenly come to you – in the bath, or by talking to other people!

Q   *Thank you.*

9 | THE WRITER AS PHOTOGRAPHER

For both staff reporters and freelance writers the ability to take good pictures to accompany a story is important. A freelance writer in particular should be able to supply good pictures when trying to sell a feature article to a magazine or newspaper. This is an integral part of the work of a freelance writer and brings in more financial reward for an article. It also requires a bit more outlay in equipment and film stock and more time involved in logging what has been taken. However, the pros far outweigh the cons and many writers welcome the challenge of taking pictures and seeing them published.

For someone who has never taken much more than snapshots on holiday, how do you take quality photographs that will catch the eye of a picture editor – and importantly – the reader.

Cameras

It is a myth that the best pictures are taken on the best equipment, and that by throwing money at expensive gear will result in good images.

Case study

Photojournalist Don McCullin's first attempt at shooting a news picture won him a contract with the *Observer* in 1958, yet it was taken with an amateur camera. The picture, of young tearaways posing arrogantly in a bombed-out building in the East End of London, accompanied a news item on the fatal stabbing of a policeman in that neighbourhood. The composition of the picture is good – everything relevant to the story is within the frame – and, most importantly, the exposure is just right. This is particularly difficult in black and white photography where the picture can be overexposed (too light in tone) or underexposed (too dark in tone). McCullin modestly attributes the correct exposure to chance, and in most good photography the element of luck is crucial for the picture to work. It was this picture that changed McCullin's life and led to him becoming one of Britain's foremost photojournalists.

The type of camera commonly used by photojournalists is known as an SLR – single lens reflex – which is a misleading descriptive term because, far from being purely single lens, the photographer can fit different lenses to the body. It is this capacity that makes it such a useful journalistic tool. The most expensive cameras are known as medium-format and large-format cameras, but these are generally used by portrait and landscape photographers. (Some photojournalists use such cameras to shoot cover pictures for magazines.)

There are various makes of SLR that can be bought on the secondhand market, and if you search the high street camera shops, there are bargains to be had. Don't be put off by a camera's age or manufacture. Provided the camera is mechanically sound, you shouldn't have a problem. An SLR made in 1970 can produce very good images and pay for itself many times over. Bear in mind that some cameras, especially those used by amateurs, will have been lovingly looked after, and probably rarely used. Cameras that have been owned by professionals, however, will have had a hard life which should show on the body of the camera in scratches and abrasions. Finally, pay special attention to the condition of the lens, which you should remove and look through. View the skin on the back of your hand through it for proof of clarity. If there is any damage in the lens by way of scratches or crystallization, these will be easy to spot.

When on assignment, it makes sense to carry at least two cameras – even three; say, two SLRs and one compact. Both SLRs should be compatible for lens fixture: with a variety of lenses to carry around, you won't want to be carrying duplicates for both cameras.

Lenses

Three lenses are normally sufficient for most assignments. These are: standard, wide angle and telephoto. If you want to become a bit more adventurous over time, invest in a zoom and a fish-eye for some incredible effects. However, concentrate on getting the basics right first.

Compact cameras have built-in lenses that focus automatically.

'I think she'll have to use a wide angle lens.'

Other equipment

A flashgun is important for illuminating objects within a specified distance of the camera, but useless beyond that distance – the light travels only so far. The flashgun is automatically activated on an SLR when the shutter opens. Most have universal fittings so that they can be attached to the shoe of any SLR.

To prevent camera shake, most photographers steady a camera on something solid, especially if they are shooting at a slow shutter speed. Photojournalists carry a telescopic monopod that will screw underneath the camera body and adjust in height. Unlike the tripod, the monopod requires minimal floor space to support a camera and can be stowed in a pocket when not in use.

Light meters are not generally used by photojournalists when shooting news pictures: by the time you have taken a reading, the picture opportunity will have passed you by. SLRs have a through-the-lens (TTL) metering system that you can see in the form of a needle through the viewfinder. You adjust the needle so that it sits centrally between the + (plus) and – (minus) icons by turning the aperture collar on the lens. In some old SLRs, the meter reading is powered by a battery; so if you are not getting a reading, replace the battery.

Film

The choice you make with regard to film is crucial for the quality of your images. An experienced picture editor can spot at a glance whether you have used a professional film or not. All the film you buy will be 35 millimetre (mm) film. This is the measured gauge of the film that fits in your camera and it is the same as that used by movie makers to shoot a film for cinematic release.

Magazines and newspapers differ in their requirements for pictures. Magazines prefer pictures to be supplied on 35 mm colour slide film (also known as colour transparencies or trannies), whilst newspapers are happier with 35 mm colour print film, which is quicker to process. That said, always check with the editor what format they require before commencing an assignment.

When taking photographs for magazines, Fujichrome Velvia colour transparency film is a preferred choice of editors and professional photographers for its fine grain and colour reproduction. Fujichrome Provia 100 is particularly good for neutral colours and is excellent when photographing people where skin tones are important. Kodachrome 64 Professional and Kodak Ektachrome also reproduce vibrant colours and fine grain. None of these professional film stocks come cheap, nor do they come in process paid packages, but by using them you will increase the saleability of your pictures and demonstrate to the target publication that you know what you are doing.

For colour negative (print) film, Kodak Vericolor VPS, VPL and VHC ranges are recommended, as are Fujicolor Super G Plus, Kodak Ektacolor Gold 160 and Kodak Ektapress.

Black and white images are rarely used by publications now, but on occasions where they are required the Agfapan ranges including 25,

100 and 400 are very good; so too are Ilford Pan F or FP4; Kodak produces Technical Pan and T-MAX 400 or 100. There is little to choose between all these very competitive and excellent films. In some cases, though, you may have to take whatever is available. Make a point of asking the editor whether the publication will process the film or whether the onus is on you. If it is, make sure you buy a film that can be processed through a photo lab if you do not do your own processing.

It is a good idea to buy film in bulk direct from the stock centres at discount prices and store in the refrigerator. This is the cheapest and most convenient way to operate.

ISO

The abbreviation ISO stands for International Standards Organization, which has replaced the American Standards Association (ASA), but shares the same arithmetical measure for film speed. The ISO number refers to the speed of the film's emulsion – in other words, its sensitivity to light. An ISO 400 is twice as fast as an ISO 200 and four times faster than an ISO 100. When choosing film for bright conditions, slower films are ideal, whilst faster films are good for overcast days and interior shots. With the better-quality films it is possible to use faster films in any given situation: many press photographers use an ISO 800, a 1600 or even a 3200. Generally, it makes sense to stick to lower speeds as these produce images of the highest quality.

When loading film into your camera, do remember to adjust the camera's film speed to that of the film, otherwise your exposures will be incorrect for the speed and you will have either overexposed or underexposed images back from the lab.

Taking pictures

The notion that good photographers can only come out of an art college degree course and then serve years in apprentice positions, is not at all true. Most publications are not looking for award-winning images, they are looking for usable pictures that are clear, concise and tell a story.

Becoming a good photojournalist is not difficult providing you follow a few simple rules that apply equally to the writer and to the photographer:

1 Always carry a camera loaded with film – everywhere you go. Even a trip out to the shops could result in seeing something newsworthy. Small compacts are ideal for carrying in a pocket.

2 At airports, place all your film in a clear plastic bag and declare it so that it does not pass through an X-ray machine. This is not always necessary but is still a good habit to get into.

3 If you are shooting at outdoor locations in summer, shoot in the early morning or late afternoon with the sun illuminating the subject.

4 Avoid taking pictures at midday when the light is fierce and people are squinting. Remember that the sun is the best light source available, so use it by keeping it behind you.

5 Use a neutralizing filter when the light is particularly bright and especially for reflective surfaces such as water.

6 When taking pictures of people in bright sunlight, to avoid their squinting place them with their backs to the sun and use a flash. This will fill-in the shadow.

7 Take a selection of near-identical shots making sure to alter the aperture on each so that you go a bit above and below the camera's in-built exposure reading. Do not be afraid to experiment by using different lenses and filters for a shot. Alter your position and that of the camera for each shot – lie on the ground and tilt the camera for effect or find a platform for an elevated shot (it might work surprisingly well).

8 Capture action and colour in your images. Pictures are about people. For a travel article, there is nothing better than a shot of people enjoying themselves. Photographers and picture editors love vibrant colours and attractive people in pictures, so include them in your shots.

9 For action shots, the subject should be moving into the frame, not out of it. Make sure the subject has plenty of room so that if the picture is cropped the subject-in-action will not be pushed against the borders of the frame.

10 Colours should harmonize, not clash. If your subject is driving a bright red sports car, they should ideally be wearing pastel colours. When shooting black and white images, contrast dark subjects against light backgrounds and vice versa.

11 Carry plenty of rolls of film and shoot lots of images. It is not unusual to shoot 140 or more images (frames) just to get half a dozen that the picture editor can use. Some work, many will not – that's photography.

12 If you do not feel confident using an SLR, use a compact. These cameras are ideal in that they automatically focus, set aperture and incorporate wide angle and zoom lenses. They are excellent for indoor photography and are used by many professional photographers.

13 Include yourself in some pictures if there is no one else around, especially when you need to show scale. Set the camera's in-built timer and be sure to wear something colourful that does not contrast with the main subject or background.

Sending pictures by post

For the freelance journalist, posting selected images to a publication is something to be treated with care. Before sending anything, it is important to have a filing system in place so that you know which pictures have been sent, when, and to whom. And you need to be aware of copyright law in respect of selling images. (More about copyright later in this chapter.) Never send pictures on the off-chance that a picture editor might use them. Always call or write, but check first.

Before posting images, make a list of what you have taken, including those that you are not sending, especially if you are keeping them on file. List them by date, title and location, and number them. Give them a code, too – one that you can make sense of as it will help you to trace pictures for future use. Over time, you will build up a personal library of images, so it makes sense to start categorizing them from the beginning.

Ideally, you should not write on photographs, although they have to be marked when compiling a list. This is where an inexpensive computer program that is designed to produce labels is well worth acquiring. Such programs offer packages that can be downloaded onto your PC for printing made-to-measure labels for transparencies (in addition to many other items). With some programs, two labels can be printed for each picture: one with your name, address and telephone number(s), the other with the title/description of the picture: Do not forget to prefix your name with a copyright mark © if you own the film and therefore hold the copyright. You can also stick these labels onto the back of prints if that is what you are sending.

When posting transparencies, slip them into the individual pockets of a special plastic folder that can be bought from stationery shops. If you are sending a large selection, loosely tie the folders with a treasury tag. Always use a purpose-made cardboard envelope capable of holding several folders.

Sending the pictures by a secure method ensures that, if they do get lost, they can be traced. If you want them returned, it is a nice gesture to include return postage, especially if you are posting to a publication abroad, in which case include an international reply coupon.

Before sealing the package, be sure to:

1 Include a letter explaining briefly the reason for sending the pictures.

2 Send copy to the features editor (or whoever requires it), not the picture editor.

3 Include a shot list itemizing each image in full, for example: Photo 2# White horse in stable, Longhorn Stables, Corsley, Wilts.

On opening the package, the picture editor will be able straight away to hold the pictures – safely contained in their plastic pockets – against a light and view them. Your labelling and packaging will not only help the editor, but also show immediately that you are no rank amateur – especially if you have not tied the treasury tag in a knot. Unless specifically requested, do not send transparencies in the little plastic boxes in which they are returned processed from the lab, as the contents can spill out across the office floor; and boxed they are not easy to file. Contained in purpose-made plastic folders, the picture editor can file them in a cabinet with all the rest – until it is time to use them.

There is another method of sending pictures which is catching on, and that is by placing the images on compact disc. This process can be done at larger high street developers or on your own PC if you have a photo scanner and the appropriate software. Before posting, always check with the editor to find out which method is preferred.

Picture copyright

Copyright, quite simply, belongs to the photographer unless the photographer is employed specifically to take photos for a publication, in other words, is a salaried press photographer working for a publication or press agency. Copyright applies to the natural lifetime of the photographer plus 50 years after their death – meaning that descendants and dependants benefit. (This may be increased for photographers resident in the EU in the near future.)

Photographers, like writers, should be aware of their responsibilities with respect to copyright:

- The freelance photographer as author holds copyright of their material and should inform clients of copyright when negotiating fees and publication.
- Contracts should be in writing and signed by both parties.
- The photographer has the right to be paid a negotiated fee for the reproduction of an image or images.
- The photographer should be identified through a published credit or byline.

If you are taking pictures as a freelance journalist, you hold the copyright unless you wish to sign over copyright to someone else. The chance of this happening is rare for most freelance journalists, but it could be that you snap what becomes an historic news event. In this respect, the picture becomes highly prized by agencies, photo libraries and publishers for syndication rights. For example, pictures of President Kennedy or the breaking down of the Berlin wall are still frequently reproduced by publications to illustrate historic events and are much sought after. If you surrender your copyright in order that your pictures are syndicated, make sure that you sign an agreement that entitles you to a fee every time the picture is published around the world.

When entering into any agreement with a client over the supply of pictures, make it clear that you hold the copyright. If you agree to surrender copyright to them, you will be losing out on substantial reproduction fees.

Do not forget, that in order to prove that you hold the copyright – should it be disputed – you should retain the negatives or similar pictures from the same batch of film.

Photographing people and places

Under British law and cultural etiquette, you are quite entitled to take pictures of people in public places. However, if you are not discrete, the possibility of upsetting someone is quite high. Under normal circumstances, always ask if you can take a picture – people are usually only too happy to oblige.

Under extreme conditions of war, emergency or riot, use your discretion and watch your back. Some of those involved might attack you as a spy, profiteer, government agent or just because you are a journalist.

When working abroad, sensitivities can be much greater regarding the taking of candid photographs of people going about their normal business in the street. Always consult the etiquette sections in travel guides for advice.

With regard to entering certain property and places to take pictures, British law prohibits trespass, that is entering private property without the permission of the owner. Pictures of private property can be taken providing the photographer is on public property at the time.

Some buildings also have automatic restrictions on photography, some of which are obvious: inside law courts, government buildings, museums and stately homes; but some of the less obvious include schools, hospitals, theatres and airports. Military establishments can be sensitive and you might find yourself surrounded by armed police and soldiers if they feel your presence poses a threat to the security of the base. If you need to take photographs in any of the above establishments, always ask permission from someone with the authority to give it – and in certain cases, get it in writing.

Finally, it is unlawful in most countries to take photographs of money and even postage stamps without permission from the National Treasury or post office respectively.

Selling pictures

Once your pictures have been published, you are quite within your rights to sell them on to other publications with the proviso that you tell them that they have already been published; in other words, you are granting them second or third rights. If they are of a very high quality, you can offer them to calendar and postcard publishers.

Rather than store lots of pictures, you can offer them to magazines that you know may be able to use them. If you intend to do this, always approach the magazine first with a letter telling them what you have. Remember that if you place your surplus pictures with a magazine, you retain copyright. So if you notice one of your pictures being used in other magazines that you have no arrangement with, or continually being used in just one, make sure that you are paid the reproduction fees for each time that the picture is used.

If your pictures are of an exceptionally high standard, you might also try placing them with a stock library. The purpose of a stock library is to supply clients with pictures, some of which will be contemporary in theme, and others archival. Owing to the demand for pictures from a worldwide range of publications, there is a constant need for libraries to supply stock pictures. Consequently, business is booming for both photographers and libraries. Some photographers make a good living out of supplying stock pictures, but the standards are high. Certain stock libraries require a minimum of 150 pictures from the photographer at the beginning of any contract, and require a further 150 or more each month depending on the original agreement. It is certainly not a way of mothballing pictures in someone else's cabinet and forgetting about them, but it can make extra money for those with ability and perseverance.

10 | FREELANCE PHOTOJOURNALISM

This chapter is aimed primarily at the freelance photojournalist, but there is plenty of information here that applies equally to the freelance writer.

There are many rewards for the freelance photojournalist. The ability to chase your own stories and choose the place where you want to work, are just two of the benefits. It is not unusual for freelances to travel the world shooting pictures for newspapers and magazines, and you do not need to be a highly trained photographer. With a lot of common sense, a desire to work and an eye for a good picture story, freelance photojournalism can become a very rewarding profession.

Before you book a flight to an exotic part of the world, consider first what is happening in your neighbourhood. Are there local papers and regional magazines that could benefit from your work? It certainly pays to approach editors and to demonstrate your abilities with a portfolio of work. Even if nothing comes of it straight away, leave your business card and keep in touch; it may be that one day the staff photographer is unable to turn up for an event and you will be given the opportunity to show your skills. In this respect, it is always a good idea to keep a mobile phone with you so that you can react to the call when it comes.

You might also consider generating your own work. The chances are that there will be something the staff photographers do not know about or cannot cover. This is where, as with all journalism, you need to make contacts in the community. Amateur dramatic and operatic societies are often fruitful venues. They not only need publicity for their next show, but also welcome a selection of photographs for their own archive and to sell to members of the society. Indeed, with amateur dramatics, you never know whether you might be photographing a star of tomorrow.

In order to sell picture stories, the ability to write – at least some words – is crucial; and that means accurately recording people's names and the parts they play. If it is amateur drama, then something along the following lines would be appropriate:

Example

Allwood Touring Players will be presenting Anton Chekhov's *The Cherry Orchard* from Thursday 15 June for three nights at the Shire Hall. Pictured from left to right: Julie Vayole (Mme Ranyevskaia); Tracy Howben (Ania); Peter Norbeen (Yephihodov). The curtain goes up at 7:45 with performances each evening. Tickets are available at the box office price £3.50 adults, £2.50 concessions, children under 16 free.

Listening to local radio news and magazine programmes is also a good way of finding out what is going on in the local area, but importantly, study the local papers to see what they like to feature with regard to pictures. It is no good setting off to photograph Mr Fred Bloggins on his allotment, and featured on a radio gardening programme, when there is nothing remarkable to snap when you get there. News pictures are about action, awards, bravery, accidents, longevity, celebrities ... If you simply take a portrait shot of Mr Bloggins leaning against his spade, that is not news. Picture him with the biggest marrow ever, or a revolutionary new spade that he has designed. *That's* news.

Unsocial hours

Keep a camera ready at all times for night shots. News does not keep office hours, so be prepared to cover stories that are breaking through the night. It could be a dramatic rescue being carried out with searchlights or a double-decker bus wedged under a low bridge. Whatever the story, the papers will want pictures.

Compacts are particularly good for work in poor light as they have automatic focus and aperture. Most importantly, make sure it is loaded with an ISO 200 colour print film.

National and international stories

Sometimes, big news will come to the journalist; most often it doesn't. If you want to break into the bigger markets covering national and international stories, do not be in too much of a hurry to leave the regions and head for the big city. London, for example, is oversubscribed with photographers, many of whom chase the rich and famous in the hope of snapping an exclusive. Besides, the chances are that on the journey up you will pass a top photojournalist heading your way to capture a breaking story that you may not have realized had greater significance.

It is not true that big things happen in big places and small things happen in small places. For example, just a couple of years ago, in the space of five days in a small Cornish town, there was a boat explosion that killed two people, a bank robbery and the fatal shooting of a local car dealer. Two of the incidents happened within one square mile, and the third related to a man who owned a showroom and garage also located within that square mile. And all this was in a sleepy little town where crime is rare.

The very fact that crime is rare in such a small town is something that you as a journalist need to recognize and exploit, as this will be part of your news angle. Imagine that these incidents have happened in your town and you call a picture editor at a national daily with a view to putting together a package. What do you think their reaction will be?

1 Great! Send us what you have straight away.
2 So what? Incidents like that happen all the time in the city.
3 What's the angle?

Either 2 or 3 is the most likely reaction from a disinterested voice who probably won't have heard of any of the incidents you are talking about or even the town – and that, at least, will be in your favour. The angle you will be pushing is that three traumatic events have taken place in the space of one week and within one mile in a quiet town where such things are normally unheard of. Not only that, but the town is a popular tourist destination and has been for much of the last century. It would make a good 'What's the world coming to?' story and might even link with a breaking story in which the government is promising to reduce crime, or similar.

For a photo story, the three incidents are problematic: you don't have any exciting footage, just the aftermath: the police clearing up the debris after the boat explosion; the garage, and the bank, both of which are unremarkable. Yet here is an amazing coincidental story that you can hardly ignore as a photojournalist – especially when it has happened on your doorstep.

A good photojournalist has to be imaginative to tell a story through pictures. Although you cannot recreate what has happened, you could ask the bank staff if they would be prepared to be photographed at the bank; take a picture of a boat similar to the one that blew up, or try to find a photo of the boat before the explosion. A few enquiries among neighbouring boat owners might bring dividends, but the family will be too traumatized to talk and it would be insensitive even to try. Shoot some general shots of the car showroom which, by using a wide angle lens with depth of field, might include in the background the area where the bank stands or even where the boat was moored. Likewise, you might be able to do similar shots of where the boat was moored showing the bank and garage in the background, or any combination of these. It would also be a good idea to include a simple map showing the close proximity of the three incidents. This can be recreated by the newspaper using a graphics program.

The text you use to link the images is vital but need not be too long: just enough to establish what happened and the connections between the bizarre series of events. Include a brief description of the town, the dates of the incidents and the reactions of local people. It is not your job to create a title, so leave that to the subeditor.

The work of a freelance is not as straightforward as that of a staff journalist: it is not enough simply to seek out and report news, which in itself is difficult enough. The freelance also has to make sense of the news if it is to be sold and understood: to convince quizzical editors and agencies of an item's news value, as they, in turn, need to sell it to their readers. The ability to spot news for a wide variety of publications is crucial, as is the ability to connect any loose pieces that make a story; pieces that might otherwise go unnoticed. It is this creative flair for news that is so important if the journalist is to function in a self-motivated, freelance environment. For example, the story of a large, ferocious pet rabbit that thinks it is a guard dog and protects its owner's property against all-comers is a small, provincial story until the freelance makes it into something bigger. The tabloids, in particular, love funny stories that show the quirky side of life, although the broadsheets are not likely to consider it.

Care also has to be taken that you do not try to promote stories to nationals when they are clearly of local interest. However, deciding what is and what is not of interest to the nationals is not easy. The battling bunny might make national news, but a supertanker on fire at the docks might not – newspapers can be very fickle.

Once you begin to sell pictures to the nationals, it is a good policy to give the papers a call every morning just to see what news may be breaking in your area. They may be interested in covering an event that you can get to easily.

The freelance photojournalist also has a worldwide market to consider when selling stories, and it would be foolhardy to think only of the national market and not consider foreign interest. Again, the battling bunny may well be an international story as well as a national one. Everyone loves a cute bunny, especially one with attitude. Ironically, the burning tanker story may well be of more interest abroad – especially in the country that owns it – than it would be to a national paper.

Press and photo agencies

It would be an expensive and time-consuming business for the freelance to call up various international papers enquiring as to whether they want pictures – especially if language is a problem. This is where press and photo agencies will do the work for you. It is in their interest to syndicate news stories, so you need to inform them of what you have and supply them with your best pictures. When supplying agencies, it is worth cultivating a good relationship as these are the people who will disperse your images to publications around the world. They might call on you for regular assignments, and this is when the money and opportunities really begin to roll in.

Supplying pictures

If you have snapped what may be a unique picture, or an exclusive, some national papers will fetch the unprocessed film from you by courier and develop it themselves – although, you will need to have convinced the editor that your picture is pretty extraordinary. If you do not process your own film, then drop it into a one-hour lab if there is one in your vicinity. Most freelances, however, have the facilities to process their own film and supply newspapers with 25 × 20 cm (10 × 8 in.) prints.

Copy should always be written to explain the picture story with brief details of who, what, where, when and how. This is where the photojournalist who can write has an advantage over a colleague who does not, though if it is breaking news, this will not be as important as the picture. Editors will accept copy by fax, e-mail or telephone.

What is a picture worth?

Most experienced photojournalists will tell you that newspapers pay a good rate for newsworthy pictures. The freelance who tries to negotiate a better price or attempts to play one paper off against another in a bidding war is likely to make themselves unpopular and unlikely to cultivate that all-important relationship which is vital for supplying pictures in the future. It is as well to remember that, across the media, people know one another and reputations can be made through hard work but broken by a greedy attitude. If you intend to stick around, do not haggle.

Equally as important: do not give anything away. You have worked hard and spent money to snap news, so make sure you are paid.

'**Do I hear 10,000 for this unique shot of Nessie? Going once, going twice ...**'

Magazines

The world's glossy magazines are a lucrative market for the freelance as the bulk of their content is normally based on colour pictures. The subject range is limitless and you do not have to find news items. This is a marvellous opportunity to indulge in your hobbies and interests as there is a magazine or two – somewhere in the world – to cater for all tastes.

Although, in many cases, magazine editors often call upon freelances they know, remember that those photojournalists also had to establish themselves. You have to do the same by promoting your work, though, as has been previously stated, do not give anything away. If your picture is printed, you must be paid for it or take action to claim your dues in the courts. If you ever have to resort to legal action, remember that you are not the first freelance to do so, nor are you likely to be the last. More about this can be found under the section 'Getting Paid' later in this chapter.

Magazines, generally, require two types of pictures: fillers, which are non-specific and can be used to fill a page with general scenes such as landscapes; and subject-related picture stories of an event. For both requirements, your timing when supplying pictures has to be just right. If you are shooting a feature on autumn breaks in Devon, you need pictures with autumnal colours and scenes: russet-coloured trees, ploughed fields and people dressed in jackets and scarves. However, you cannot supply them in autumn as the magazine is put together months in advance. You need to get material to the editor by June or July for an autumn issue. Much depends on whether the magazine is published weekly, monthly or quarterly. Whichever, contact the editor in good time with your suggestion – at least three to four months in advance.

In respect of seasonal features, you need to plan 12 months ahead by shooting images for use in next year's issue. This can work well providing you follow up to make sure that what you shot last year is still relevant this year. The problem could arise that the quaint old pub you shot nestling in the valley last year, has either burnt to the ground in the interim or closed and is now boarded up. There is nothing an editor hates more than having irate readers contact the magazine to say that the place they sought out for a weekend autumn break on the strength of your feature, no longer exists. Most editors are very trusting in accepting freelance features and will assume that you did your research thoroughly, and have since checked to see that everything is still as you said it was.

Originality is much sought after, although this should not be confused with avant-garde work that does not fit the magazine's style. Consider your target magazine carefully, and a subject angle that would complement, but not clash, with the normal contents. A fresh angle is always welcome from both editor and readers, and the onus is on the freelance to be creative and to find something new.

This is probably easier in the general subject magazines as opposed to the specialists. Shooting a piece on the restoration of a veteran motorcycle for a superbike magazine is hardly likely to sell; there are specialist magazines for classic motorcycle owners. However, offer the piece on the veteran motorcycle to some general-readership magazines, and the chances are you will have a sale. A certain amount of luck is also involved: if the editor happens to be a motorcycle fanatic, your job will be much easier.

Of course, there are plenty of exceptions and few golden rules. In-house and trade magazines will take an item that is not subject-related to their title providing the item has some relevance. A magazine for teachers might welcome a piece on hill-walking in Snowdonia; or a builder's trade magazine might take a photo story on fishing or amateur photography.

Likewise, when it comes to travel pictures, try to find the as yet undiscovered or forgotten places. It would be pointless trying to sell an item on clubs and pubs in Tenerife, although the hidden churches of Tenerife might sell many times over.

A photojournalist probably has more scope for supplying material to magazines than a writer. Pictures sell in any language and do not need translation. And there is no limit to the subjects you could cover: it might be a piece on British telephone boxes or even light bulbs down the century. If it exists, it needs to be photographed.

Approaching editors

When approaching magazine editors, it is better to start with a preliminary letter introducing yourself and what you have to offer. Do not send any original prints at this point, although, there is nothing to stop you including a small colour print as part of the design in your letterheading. If your PC is connected to a colour laser printer, you will be able to reproduce your best pictures on A4 sheets. You can also include a business card that displays your pictures as part of the design.

Later, when you are established and known by the staff, by all means call and discuss ideas. However, to begin with, write.

Contracts

Where possible, before embarking on a self-financed assignment, and especially before submitting any pictures, get a contract. This need only be an acknowledgement from the publication agreeing to accept 'X' amount of pictures which will be paid at such-and-such a rate upon publication. You cannot ask for a contract if you are simply sending in material on spec, but if it is agreed between you that material will be used in a forthcoming edition, then ask for the agreement in writing. The contract can be in the form of an e-mail.

If this sounds a bit cheeky coming from a beginner, just say that it helps you to keep records of what has been sent – which it will – and makes it clear for both parties what is required and when. Otherwise, you could find yourself at loggerheads with an editor who says: 'I wanted so-and-so yesterday, not the day after!'

Do not be inclined to send pictures before receiving written confirmation unless you are placing stock pictures with the magazine on an arrangement where they can use them as and when the need arises.

Sometimes a magazine will agree to publish your work and then cancel it – often without informing you. This is sometimes prompted by the arrival of a new editor who sweeps all before them. In such cases, you are entitled to what's known as a kill fee. This compensates you for having had your time and effort wasted and should be followed up by you as editors will not volunteer it. The kill fee probably will not compensate you to the value that you would have been paid on publication, but at least you are free to offer the work with first rights attached to any other publication. Unfortunately for you, by that time, it is all too late.

Rates for the job

You will need to talk rates with the editor when agreeing to supply pictures. Even if it is your first commission, do not admit as much. Never proclaim or excuse yourself as a beginner. This does not mean that you have to lie, nor will you be asked to, simply go about selling your work in the way you mean to carry on: with enthusiasm, professionalism, dedication and spirit. No editor will know it is your first commission – unless you tell them so.

It is usually left to the freelance to bring rates into the conversation. The editor may hope that you are offering something for free. Make sure there is no ambiguity and raise the issue by asking what rates are paid and how soon after publication. Find out beforehand what the standard industry rates are, and do not agree to less. If you do, you are diminishing the value of your work and consequently that of your colleagues who will find it more and more difficult to receive the going rate for the job, especially if editors think they can get away with paying less.

Rates also depend on the size of picture you are supplying and the place it will occupy in the magazine. For example, a half-page, double-page or even cover spread, all have varying rates and you need to seek advice if you are not sure what to charge. Do not give in to an editor who wants to use your picture on the cover but is not prepared to pay the going rate because they do not have the available budget. The NUJ publishes guidelines on picture rates for its members (see Chapter 20).

When you sell pictures to magazines, you are selling rights for the pictures to be published in one edition only. If the pictures reappear in the magazine in any other issue, you must be paid for reproduction. The pictures are not being bought *from* you. The magazine has no right to pass or sell your pictures on to someone else without consultation and gaining your permission first. On your part, you cannot offer the same pictures to other magazines, although you can offer similar ones.

Getting paid

Keep up-to-date records of what has been sent to whom, and where, and invoice promptly when your pictures have been published. Few, if any, publications will send a cheque for dues unless they have been invoiced. Slow payers should be avoided when it comes to future assignments: the chances are that they are in financial trouble and cannot meet payments. You can try including a penalty clause which states that for every week or month they delay, you charge them interest, but this is unlikely to be met as they know that to make a case out of it, you would have to go to a lot of time, trouble and expense.

If payment is not forthcoming, send a warning with a deadline for payment, stating that if payment is not received then you will have no choice but to start an action in the county court – commonly referred to as the 'Small Claims Court'. This method of redress for non-payment is easier and cheaper to initiate than most people imagine. It does not involve hiring a solicitor and putting together a strong case that will go before a magistrate, although you should have proof that you entered into a contract with the publication and that they have reneged on payment. This is where it pays to ensure you have a letter from the editor agreeing to 'X' amount of pictures to be paid at such-and-such a rate upon publication.

Once you've started ('issued') your claim, the court will post the publication (as 'defendant') with a 'response pack' on your behalf as the 'plaintiff'. This is usually enough to cause the publication to pay up and, if you win your case, means they also have to pay the cost of your action, the value of which will depend upon the amount you are claiming. Do not concern yourself over losing a client; if they couldn't or wouldn't pay, you haven't lost anything.

Study the magazine market carefully. Understand that some magazines are very short-lived and soon disappear from the market, often taking journalists' dues with them – staff as well as freelance. It is one thing to launch a magazine, but to keep it going amongst strong competition is very difficult. If you are in too much of a hurry to supply material to a newly launched magazine, prepare to have your fingers burnt. The best advice is: do not supply until you are sure, through recommendation at least, that the magazine is a long-term fixture on the shelves and that the editor will honour contributors.

Finding markets for your work

One of the few downsides of working as a freelance is the wait for money to come through paying you in full for an assignment: but if publication is held up, there is little that can be done about it. You can ask to have your material returned so that you can sell it elsewhere, but this does not help to establish your credentials with that publication. In most cases, it is as well to grin and bear it.

To avoid being caught out by such things, make a habit of working daily to build up a full-time business. If you are just going to wait around for the cheque to drop on the mat each time you do a job, you will only ever be a part-timer. As soon as you have completed one project and put it in the post, work on the next. A year later, you should have cheques dropping on your mat on a regular basis.

Set yourself a target each week for supplying magazines or papers with pictures. If you are shooting a piece for a particular magazine, there is nothing to stop you selling a similar piece to other publications provided you supply original material for each and inform editors of what you have already sold. Be sure to record everything you photograph, send and sell, so nothing gets misplaced or forgotten.

As your freelance career develops, you may find yourself specializing or catering for many diverse markets. The relationship you build up with a local or even national paper could mean working regular assignments for them to the exclusion of all else. This may result in your working like a staff photographer, but without employment benefits such as sick pay and holiday entitlement. In this case, it might be worth reconsidering your position and ask to be taken on as a full-time salaried member of staff. Whatever the nature of freelance work you do, be sure to inform your local tax office.

The bulk of your work may be for press agencies or public relations companies – the latter provide some excellent opportunities for the freelance. If you do intend to work for a public relations company, invest in a good medium- or large-format camera, as high-quality pictures are essential. Indeed, larger-format cameras are a worthwhile investment once you are established especially if you want your shots to grace the front covers of magazines.

If you intend to use larger-format cameras, you should consider providing pictures for postcards, calendars and stock images. These are well worth following up but require a great deal of work and determination if you are to become established.

Finally, you may want to consider joining that rare breed of freelance photojournalist who stalks new models of car during development trials by the manufacturer. Their customers are chiefly the car magazines and the financial rewards for top pictures are high. The drawbacks in this line of work are the long searches to find where a car is being tested – which could be anywhere in the world; the endless waiting – often perched high in a tree; and especially the antagonism from other photojournalists who are well established in the field and will not welcome seeing you perched alongside them.

For the contact book

BJP Market Newsletter
Bureau of Freelance Photographers
Focus House
497 Green Lanes
London N13 4BP
Tel: 020 8882 3315
Fax: 020 8886 5174
E-mail: info@thebfp.com
Internet: www.bfp.com

Freelance Focus
7 King Edward's Terrace
Brough
East Yorks HU15 1EE
Tel: 01482 666036

Enquiries write:
Freepost (HU593)
Brough HU15 1BR
(No stamp required)

The Freelance Photographer's Market Handbook
Bureau of Freelance Photographers
Focus House
497 Green Lanes
London N13 4BP
Tel: 020 8882 3315
Fax: 020 8886 5174
E-mail: info@thebfp.com
Internet: www.bfp.com

See also:

- *Writers' and Artists' Yearbook* (Black, published annually)
- *The Writer's Handbook 2000* (Macmillan, 1999)
- *Willing's Press Guide 2000* (Hollis Directories Ltd, published anually)

Books

Lee Frost, *Taking Pictures For Profit*. David & Charles, 1996
Contents include: the road to freelancing; making contact; record-keeping; the magazine market; selling to newspapers; and much more.

11 | PHOTOJOURNALISM

The picture is almost invariably read first; the common habit is for the reader's eyes to move back and forth from picture to words and back again until the meaning expressed in each medium is completely understood.

Wilson Hicks, 1973

The word 'photojournalism' was coined in 1924 by Frank Luther Mott of the University of Missouri School of Journalism, to describe someone who can combine the skills of the photographer with those of being a reporter. The term 'press photographer' is also commonly used in media circles but does not describe the same job. In addition to taking the picture, the press photographer is responsible for getting the caption information accurate, particularly people's names.

They say a picture is worth a thousand words. They certainly help to convey a story by illuminating a scene through imagery. A picture complements text, as text in turn complements the picture. This seems to be a good working partnership as visual image and text document corroborates the evidence of the other. Pictures at first glance appear to be a reflection of reality, though it is important to consider that within any picture the overall truth surrounding an event can remain elusive. Pictures are less than perfect records for many reasons, not least because they are limited by the frame, they are two-dimensional, and because they are taken from one person's viewpoint.

Photojournalists talk of the need to have 'all-round vision' when first surveying a scene. Most important is the general view shot which is the equivalent of the cinematographer's master shot. It is the shot that shows the scene in its entirety before closer shots of specific details are taken. Often, and because of sensitivity in using shots that show badly injured people or bodies, the general view is the one most used by picture editors as it helps to sum up answers to the many questions the reader will ask when viewing the published picture: Where did it happen? How many people were involved? How big was the accident? The general view helps to show something of the scale, especially if people are in it.

As a matter of practice, many photojournalists carry a camera with them at all times, even when they are off-duty. This is always good policy as a news story can happen at anytime and anywhere. The first images of the Brixton pub bombing in April 1999 were captured by a photographer who was shopping nearby at the time. He was able to take pictures before the emergency services arrived even though there was a danger that a second bomb might have been due to explode. However, photography remains an imprecise art and so it is not until pictures are developed that usable images can be identified. These can arise as much out of happenstance as from skill or experience. In an unexpected event, a photographer cannot pose his subjects and needs to be able to react instinctively to what is happening.

Importantly, when carrying a camera, always make sure that it is loaded with a fresh roll of film – never keep a half-used roll of film in a camera. A compact is useful in these situations as it focuses automatically, meaning the photographer does not need to spend time adjusting the aperture or changing lenses.

An image does not need to be one of blood and gore in order to tell a story of horror. Indeed, if a picture is too graphic in detail showing badly injured or dead people, it will not be used by the mainstream press. Photographers can come under attack in situations where people have been killed or injured. In the mayhem that follows an accident or disaster, the sight of a photographer shooting pictures of people laying wounded or dead can be enough to incite survivors and bystanders to attack them for what appears to be intrusion into grief with the intention of profiteering from a tragedy. And yet, sometimes it is these attacks, verbal or physical, that can add an extra element to the picture.

Case study

Photographer Dave Trainer's black and white picture of two men tending to an injured friend lying on the wet street was used by most of the Fleet Street press in their coverage of the Brixton bombing. What makes the picture so strong an image is that the man giving first aid looks and points – accusingly – at the camera. The anger in the wake of the devastation caused by the bomb is immediately captured with the man's gesture and expression.

The starkness of the image can be accentuated by its being in black and white. Black and white also neutralizes the colour of blood which, if photographed in colour, might render a picture unusable owing to the sensitivity surrounding the use of graphic images.

Under such circumstances, a photographer does not approach a person for permission to take their photograph or follow up by asking their identity although discreet enquiries can be made about the condition of an injured person and a follow-up story can arise out of this.

Case study

Soon after the collision between two passenger trains at Paddington in November 1999, police enforced an exclusion zone around the crash site and which extended 2,000 feet skywards with the specific aim of preventing aerial shots. In a situation such as this, journalists oblige by remaining outside exclusion zones. Because the accident scene was largely out of view from street level, an aerial, or at best elevated, shot, was the most desired by picture editors. Remarkably, photographer Marco Deidda's flat overlooked the crash scene and he was able to take some of the first shots of the overturned, burning carriages, and survivors climbing out of the wreckage. Deidda followed up with further shots taken from ground level before calling the *Evening Standard* who immediately processed the film. Again, it was the general shot taken from his flat window that was considered most important as it gave perspective and scale. Other shots showed the humanitarian aspect of rescue services carrying survivors to waiting ambulances. A delicate balance is required: the public need to know the extent of, and horror surrounding, the disaster. But the combination of images and text should not cause grief for readers with material that contains nothing but shock value. Therefore, pictures of heroic rescue workers and survivors are counterbalanced with shots of flames and palls of smoke rising from the wreckage.

This is not to say that graphic images are not used in other newspapers around the world. In Sri Lanka, for example, where a civil war has been raging for many years, newspapers have printed on their front pages, and in colour, horrifyingly graphic pictures of the remains of Tamal Tiger bombers who had strapped explosives to their bodies and committed suicide in the streets.

What causes journalists to bow to unwritten conventions in the reportage of wars and disasters?

The Vietnam War

In the case of war, many of these unwritten conventions had been formed through coverage of the US military involvement in Vietnam between the years 1962 (with the deployment of the first advisers) to 1975. The Vietnam War saw an unprecedented increase in the use of graphic news material that left an indelible impression on the minds of people around the world. Among the many thousands of images shot and published between 1962 and 1975, the most notable of these were of the Buddhist monk who set himself alight in a street protest against the war (1963); the public execution of a Vietcong man after the Tet Offensive (1969); the My Lai massacre (published 1969); and, towards the end of the war, the small girl running from a napalm bomb attack, her skin badly burned (1972).

Although the war was largely televised, it was the pictures syndicated across the world's press that left the greatest impression. The role of the photojournalist in war is the most difficult of all, and certainly the most dangerous. Journalism's purpose is defined by its practitioners as one that captures the misery of war for all those involved without being partisan. The photojournalist's job is to present images that will portray as accurate a story as possible of the conditions being suffered.

Even before full-scale US involvement in what had already been a long war of liberation from French colonial power, press agencies in Vietnam were wiring the American press with some of the most horrific images of the effects of modern warfare on the civilian population. The most evocative of these was that of the burning monk, taken by Malcolm Browne. The use of such horrific images between 1962 and 1965 by the western press was sporadic, with war reporters such as James Cameron and American, Harrison Salisbury, vilified as traitors in the West. Despite this, it became the aim of the agencies based in South Vietnam to bring the war to the attention of people across the world, especially as the USA was sending some of its first military advisers during this period. Browne's photograph of the burning monk was even seen on President John F. Kennedy's desk in the Oval Office at the White House. Ironically, this photograph may have prompted Kennedy to send more troops.

For many war photographers, the decision to take photographs of death and the grief of others is one that is very hard to live with. It is not easy to justify such a personal intrusion into the grief of other human beings. In 1970, photojournalist Larry Burrows said in a television interview for the BBC programme *Omnibus*:

> *So often I wonder whether it is my right to capitalize, as I feel so often, on the grief of others. But then I justify my own particular thoughts by feeling that if I can contribute a little to the understanding of what others are going through, then there's reason for doing it.'*

(Larry Burrows was killed with several other journalists when the helicopter he was travelling in was shot down over Laos in 1971.)

Although the American press had initially viewed involvement in Vietnam as being generally acceptable (it was presented as a moral crusade), by the time of the Tet Offensive in 1969, the frequent publication of pictures showing dead, dying and wounded US soldiers was enough to turn the tide of public opinion. But it was the picture of a man being publicly executed in the streets of Saigon that did more than any other image to convince the American public that the war in Vietnam was no moral crusade.

The Execution, as it became titled, was taken by photojournalist Eddie Adams, who, at the moment of taking the picture, had no idea that the prisoner would be shot in front of his camera lens. The execution was also filmed and broadcast on television news across the world, but it was the lasting effect of the black and white picture that most profoundly affected public opinion. To the American public, the gruesome picture in which a South Vietnamese general executes a man without trial was unacceptable. This picture, probably more than any other, turned the tide of press and public opinion against the war. The bulk of American troops in Vietnam were withdrawn shortly after due largely to vigorous protests in the USA and around the world to bring American involvement in Vietnam to a close.

Despite the best efforts of photojournalists and press agencies in Vietnam, a large majority of graphic images – especially those showing Vietnamese victims of the war – were never published. The gruesome images of terrified civilians, mostly women and children, huddled together before being shot in ditches at the village of My Lai, were not published until a year after the event.

During the Vietnam War, western journalists had found it very easy to gain access to any and all areas of combat in Vietnam. They were accredited by the American Defense Department (regardless of nationality – many were British) and given an honorary commissioned rank. They could then choose a helicopter from a daily flight line (much like hailing a taxi from a rank) and fly out to join a combat platoon engaged on a mission. Unarmed, photojournalists said they often felt protected, and shielded by their cameras from the bullets and horrors of battle. There were no restrictions imposed on what could be reported or photographed and, on returning to base, journalists were frequently billeted in officer's quarters.

The price paid by journalists for this freedom, however, was high. Some 200 journalists covering both sides of the war, and of all nationalities, were killed, whilst others were wounded or captured.

For those that survived the war, the transition to more peaceful assignments often proved difficult as the psychological damage took its toll. In Saigon today, a small memorial built by a Vietnamese photojournalist is the only memorial to those journalists who lost their lives.

Never again was war so freely covered by western journalists or such graphic images used to convey brutality.

'Impossible' images

One of the most common television news pictures is that of press photographers holding their cameras up to the darkened windows of prison vans in a vain attempt to snap a 'lucky' image of the occupants being driven away from court to begin a custodial sentence. More often than not, these attempts to snap a criminal result in nothing more than an unusable black frame. Inside, the van is made up of separate compartments and the photographer has no way of knowing which compartment the prisoner is in. Also, the black film covering the windows reflects the flashlight and is designed specifically to stop photographers getting an image. This attempt to get a photograph is often a last resort, but one still worth following up.

Case study

One shot through a prison van window was usable after a lot of 'cleaning up' on the computer. Disgraced politician Jonathan Aitken was snapped by Press Association photographer Michael Walter when Aitken was being taken away to begin his sentence. Reflections had also been caught but were magically removed with the aid of a PC photo program and the rest of the image cropped leaving a clear image of the prisoner inside the van on his way to begin his sentence.

Celebrity pictures

Not all news picture stories are of accidents and disasters. Celebrity weddings are prearranged with the media who will pay – often substantial sums – to cover the wedding exclusively. Celebrities who wish to marry in private without announcement, are rarely harried by the press unless a tip-off is given by an insider. Covering celebrity weddings has become the preserve of magazines such as *Hello!* and its rival *OK!* who try to outbid one another for exclusive rights, and often to the cost of Fleet Street newspapers. The magazines not only make a large payment, but also organize parts of the wedding including the provision of security that effectively keeps other journalists from getting pictures and stories. Such zealous precautions, however, can often backfire as Fleet Street retaliates with snatched shots and stories of heavy-handed security guards and public relations staff – all of which reflects badly on the celebrities in the public eye.

Case study

Radio One DJ Zoe Ball's marriage to Fat Boy Slim star Norman Cooke provided press photographers with a specially arranged photo session in which the couple happily kissed and caressed before the cameras. This kept Fleet Street happy and gave excellent press coverage to the story. The couple's open arrangement with the press, planned in advance, prevented intrusive opportunist shots and no deal was struck for an exclusive. Picture desk editors were forewarned and prepared a week ahead for a photo-call so that everyone was ready for the big day. The colour pictures run the following morning showed a happy couple of newly-weds. This particular wedding was a fine example of how to get on with the press.

Sports pictures

When the rematch between Britian's Lennox Lewis and the USA's Evander Holyfield was annouced in 1999, for the heavyweight boxing title of the world, sports journalists in both countries were prepared. Because the fight was to be staged in America, it meant that the Saturday editions of British papers had already gone to press.

For such a large sporting event, plenty of provision is made for photographers and reporters with fight promoters allocating various ringside and even overhead positions, and a nearby press room with computer terminals. The idea is to provide photojournalists with as many advantageous views of the ring as possible. However, an allocated position does not allow a photographer the freedom to cover other parts of the event and so there is little room for movement. It's a bit like buying a ticket to the theatre; if you're stuck in a bad position, there's nothing that can done about it and so the photographer is very reliant on luck for a good shot.

As the fight gets under way, photographers wait to see which way the fight is going before shooting. In this instance, an establishing general shot is not necessary. However, shots of action from the fight and the eventual winner with gloved fist raised make great picture stories. This is very much convention. Action pictures are all important: a blow to the head, or even an expression of anguish on the face of the combatants. Once one boxer begins to dominate, the focus is then on him. Good action pictures are determined by a fraction of a second. So fast is the movement of the boxers, it's impossible to calculate through a viewfinder just what will be a good shot. Again, luck plays a big part. Indeed, the adage goes, 'If you see it in your viewfinder, you've missed it.'

All successful sports pictures rely heavily on the element of luck, although luck can be increased through capable and experienced hands and the choice of highly professional equipment. Luck in itself does not detract from the photographer's ability, as both elements must be present in order for a picture to work.

Once the action is over, then the shot of the victor (and the disappointed loser) are good useable shots for picture editors, but it is that elusive action shot that is crucial for a good picture story. Sports photographers are often looking for a shot that is in no way clichéd: the glove landing on the chin, or the ball kicked straight into the net. It is the elusive moment where an expression of determination is captured within a particular setting or atmosphere. Of the many thousands of frames that are shot, only one will tell the story.

For the contact book

Association of Photographers
9/10 Domingo Street
London EC1 0TA
Tel: 020 7739 6669
Fax: 020 7739 8707
E-mail: aop@dircon.co.uk
Internet: www.aophoto.co.uk

British Institute of Professional Photography
Amwell End
Ware
Hertfordshire SG12 9HN
Tel: 01920 464011
Fax: 01920 487056
E-mail: bipp@compuserve.com
Internet: www.bipp.com

Books

Martin Keene, *Practical Photojournalism – A Professional Guide* (2nd edition). Focal Press, 1995
Contents include: The working photographer; captions; law; careers; the picture desk; and much more.

Ken Kobre, *Photojournalism – A Professional Approach* (3rd edition). Focal Press, 1995
Contents include: cameras and film; general news; picture stories; editing; the law; features; sport, and much more.

Jon Tarrant, *Professional Press, Editorial and PR Photography*, Focal Press, 1998
Contents include: camera equipment; working to a brief; career spotlights; and much more.

12 | THE PRESS PHOTOGRAPHER

The role of the press photographer carries immense responsibility. Whereas a writer can meet their subject face-to-face and pose questions before using a variety of words to describe the story, the photographer has a much more difficult task when reporting news. The picture is the photographer's one and only 'statement'; and if the picture does not develop, it is too late to turn around and ask if it can be done again.

The photographer is also more vulnerable to attack in situations of riot or war; yet remains hidden behind the camera when confronting the subject. This notion of being hidden can make the photographer feel invulnerable, as if the camera were a shield protecting them from the world directly in front of the lens.

Of course, not all press photography revolves around war and riot. Indeed, most press photographers never encounter such drama. The bulk of a photographer's work features the everyday lives of the ordinary person in the news, and the celebrity. With regard to the latter, it might be said that without the photographer, there would be much less by way of celebrity, as the image can glamorize those who might otherwise be considered unremarkable.

No sooner has one photographic assignment been accomplished, than it is time to shoot the next. The daily work of the press photographer can have what seems like an unending succession of tasks that may not be completely satisfying. For the creative photographer who wants to make a more personal statement, any desire for individual creativity has to be subsumed – at least until the end of the working day. And yet, amongst the drudgery of the mundane, news being what it is, the exciting appears as if out of nowhere and the press photographer, like all journalists, can be faced with a monumental challenge.

In this chapter, the term 'press photographer' is used as opposed to photojournalist. In essence, both terms describe the same profession, but for the purpose of defining the specific role of the salaried press photographer working directly as a member of staff for a newspaper, 'press photographer' will be used so as not to be confused with the contents of Chapter 11 on freelance photojournalism.

Essential training

The press photographer is at something of a disadvantage to the reporter, in that the press photographer has to have all the inherent ability that goes with being a journalist, plus the ability to recognize a good news picture before pressing the shutter and developing the results.

The number of press photographers employed as salaried members of a paper's staff has diminished in recent years and career vacancies are not as numerous as those for writers. There are two main factors behind this: cost cutting, and the introduction of multiskilling. Reporters on some papers are given a camera and asked to take pictures in addition to their normal duties. Freelance photographers and press agencies have also filled the gaps left by staff photographers.

In this respect, the aspirant press photographer has to plan a career strategy very carefully before applying for training courses and that first job. The irony is that the demand for high-quality colour pictures is probably greater now than it has ever been. Likewise, the demand from those wishing to join the ranks of working journalists has also never been greater, so the competition is fierce.

It helps to think ahead and to imagine how your career might develop over a lifetime. Consider the papers you want to work for, the people you want to work with and the places you want to see.

Editors recruit press photographers from applicants who have either recently passed a pre-entry NCTJ course in photojournalism, or are able to undertake a probationary course as a direct entrant straight from school or university, leading up to the NCTJ National Certificate. For those undertaking courses whilst working for a newspaper, block-release periods are spent at college learning theory and completing practical assignments in photography, law, newspaper practice and caption-writing. Tests after each module ensure that the candidate passes each subject before going on to take the National Certificate, which is awarded at the end of the course. Candidates have to present a portfolio of coursework that demonstrates their ability as a photographer and complete timed assignments that replicate the demands of daily work. Some newspaper groups run in-house training schemes, which means that candidates can apply directly to the editors of those papers.

To undertake an NCTJ course as a direct entrant from school or college, candidates should ideally have four GCSEs (grades A to C) including English, or the equivalent GNVQs. Pre-entry candidates should possess the above qualifications plus an additional 'A' level. Mature applicants coming to the course from other professions should demonstrate a relevant ability and experience in either photography or communications if they do not possess any of the qualifications mentioned above.

Those unable to secure an initial job with a newspaper may wish to join a pre-entry course under the NCTJ scheme. Candidates should possess a minimum of one 'A' level and four GCSEs (one of which should be in English), or equivalent GNVQs. The course covers much the same content as the probationary block-release schemes, with students applying for trainee posts on newspapers at the end of an 18-month training contract. The National Certificate is taken once a job is secured and the candidate has spent at least 18 months working with the paper. Details for the NCTJ are listed at the end of this chapter.

Portfolios

Before any approach is made to an editor, a portfolio of work should be put together to demonstrate your knowledge of photography and general ability. Pictures should, ideally, reflect journalistic themes: the fire brigade rescuing a cat from a tree perhaps, or a football match with action shots taken from the touchline. School or college leavers could put together a photo story of academic events, from sports days to visiting VIPs and awards ceremonies. Mature applicants should put together a varied portfolio of black and white, and colour images, each of which relates to a people-in-the-news theme. Landscapes or portraits, however well presented, might suggest the candidate is a fine photographer but not necessarily a journalist in the making.

Putting together a portfolio takes time, effort and some expense. The best portfolios combine prints and transparencies presented in a folder that can be leafed through easily. Prints should be mounted on white card which can be inserted into the clear plastic sheets of the folder. Folders should be specifically for displaying pictures and bought from a specialist outlet such as an art supplies shop or photographer, who can also advise on the best ways to present work.

If you have pictures that have been published, then these should also be included as tearsheets – cuttings or photocopies of the original published pages. If you have a lot of tearsheets, a specially-made pro-book can be bought. Although expensive they are well worth the investment when demonstrating your professionalism to a prospective employer.

Colour transparencies can be presented in transparent sheets that have special pockets in which the slides can be placed. Sheets can then be placed in a file for easy viewing. Black mask sheets can be bought to display pictures taken on larger-format cameras that produce 6 × 6 cm slides. Caption each picture if you can by using a special labelling program that you can download onto your PC.

Simply by presenting your pictures in a professional manner, you will be showing an editor that you know not only how to take good photographs, but how to present images as well. This is particularly important in journalism, as the presentation of images is crucial if the message behind the picture is to come across.

Do not be tempted to cut corners by presenting photocopies of your work. With the exception of tearsheets, include in your portfolio 20 to 30 of your original and best images. Keep updating them with your current work, and make sure they are relevant to journalism. Think about why you consider them your best images, so that when asked why a certain picture has worked for you, you can explain whatever it is about the tones, composition or subject.

Finally, do not be overconfident by including self-written 'news' captions as if you were presenting real photo-stories. The editor will be much more interested in the composition of your pictures and understands that you will learn the art of writing news captions on your course.

The job interview

When presenting yourself, do be sure to arrive for your interview in good time, at the right place, and knowing the title and name of the person(s) who will interview you and their position on the paper, for example Ms Smyth, Picture Editor. Dress smartly and formally – not combat gear or in Chinos and a photographer's waistcoat, pockets bulging with film and lenses. If you are successful and taken on, it is important that you maintain a smart appearance at all times as you will be representing the paper wherever you are sent. Unless you have been asked to bring a camera or two with you, there should be no need to come with cameras draped around your neck, though you might want to stick a compact in your coat pocket to demonstrate that you are always ready to snap a newsworthy shot. (Make sure it is loaded so that you can talk about the reasons why a compact is useful and why you chose such-and-such a film.) Importantly, do not call the interviewer by their first name, however friendly they might seem. The best policy is to avoid using people's names in either formal or informal terms. Just be as bright and attentive as possible – as journalists should be.

Magazines

Magazines offer unique opportunities to photographers setting out on their career. Staff positions are usually with the larger, well-established publications that specialize in a particular subject. There are great opportunities to be had provided you are happy snapping feature pictures rather than news pictures.

The picture desk

On newspapers, photographers work directly under the supervision of a picture editor or chief photographer who in turn is directly responsible to the editor. Depending on the size of the newspaper, the picture desk can comprise a team where deputy and assistant editors manage a host of duties from running the diary (where assignments for photographers are posted), to supplying photographic equipment, selecting pictures, developing, cropping and cleaning up pictures, and liaising with freelances, agencies and other departments. The smaller the paper, the smaller the picture desk, but the work is the same.

The picture desk does not work in isolation from the newsdesk: both news and picture editors need to liaise in a concerted effort to find stories and report them. They frequently share the same office.

Assignments

Generally, a photographer is assigned a job on the strength of prearranged events. The diary lists occasions where pictures are required. Even during rather mundane events, the photographer will be looking out for the unusual.

A good picture editor will place a photographer in a situation where the photographer's strengths and interests are best served. There is no advantage to be had in sending a photographer to cover a football match if they do not know or care much about the sport.

Mobile phones keep the photographer in touch with the newsdesk and have become an essential tool in keeping both parties informed of developing stories. When a hard news story breaks, the picture editor has to decide instantly who to pull from one job and send to cover the story. Often the choice will be down to who is nearest, but the call will also go out to freelances whose work the editor knows.

The photographer has to use a lot of common sense when arriving at the scene of a major accident or catastrophe where people have lost their lives and others are injured. In such a situation, chaos reigns. There is no one around to guide the photographer; to the contrary, the last thing anybody in the emergency services wants to see is a press photographer getting in the way of rescue operations. The best policy is to consult the picture desk by phone (if possible) and look for a vantage point where you can take photographs whilst not getting in anyone's way. In reality, you could be charged with obstruction if you do get in the way.

Some of the sights you see will be deeply distressing and the chances are that nothing in your experience will have prepared you for the gruesome scenes of carnage. Even the most experienced of photographers can be deeply traumatized by what they witness. When covering riots, the level of violence surrounding photographers who need to be on the street is frightening and the chances of being attacked are high. This may be because the rioters mistakenly consider you as an agent of the police force or government. After all, your photographs may identify them and result in a prison sentence. In such a situation, try to find cover where you can see what is going on whilst not exposing yourself to attack, stray missiles and flying debris.

Agencies

Agencies employ a mix of staff and freelance photographers. To work as an agency photographer, you need to be fully trained with an NCTJ qualification or equivalent. Competition for posts is high and you will be competing with freelances, so you need to be good at your job. If you are late for assignments or fail to produce the goods, the agency will probably dispense with your services much more quickly than an editor would. Pay scales are not always as good as on newspapers, though if your standard of work is high, the rewards too will be high.

The larger, international agencies such as Reuters or Associated Press provide a lot of international coverage and therefore assign photographers to posts around the world. This may at first sound glamorous, but the dangers mixed with the tedium of some overseas postings can counter the initial enthusiasm. Marriages and partnerships can suffer owing to long absences, and it is no fun when you are hungry, thirsty, jet-lagged and the climate is too hot or too cold. However, for the single and adventurous photographer, overseas postings can be the greatest experience in your career, and may be the inspiration behind wanting to join the profession in the first place.

If you do intend to pursue a career that takes you abroad frequently, it pays to able to speak more than one language. If you can speak Spanish, French and German to a competent degree and have a good understanding of various cultures, you could find yourself in demand for foreign assignments.

Smaller agencies working in the provinces employ their own staff photographers to cover stories where papers cannot get one of their own staff to quickly. The agency will be contracted by the paper to supply 'X' number of pictures as quickly as possible. Often, the agency will be ahead of breaking news in their area and will automatically cover stories that they will then try to sell to the newspapers. They are working in competition with freelances and regional newspapers who might also be able to supply a paper with the pictures they need. There is no such thing as loyalty when it comes to buying the right pictures.

Training opportunities

For further information on training to be a press photographer, contact:

National Council for the Training of Journalists (NCTJ)
Latton Bush Centre
Southern Way
Harlow
Essex CM18 7BL
Tel: 01279 430009
Fax: 01279 438008
E-mail: NCTJTraining@aol.com
Internet: http://www.nctj.com

13 TELEVISION NEWS (1)

Ever since news was first broadcast on BBC television in 1954, when only the voice of the newsreader could be heard over the display of photographs, maps and captions, there has been a series of changes in the way that news is presented. As in print and radio, these changes have been due to the implementation of new working practices and technology combined with a growing demand for more and more news broadcasts. Today, some 80 per cent of the population turn to the television as their main source of news. Audiences have put greater trust into the content of television news than radio – seemingly on the basis that what the eye sees must be true.

Most news organizations, such as the BBC, ITN, CNN and Sky News, are subject to pressures of which the viewing public remain blissfully unaware. The aim of broadcasting news is not simply to convey the stories making news, but to attract audience figures, too. Just like the newspapers who need to keep circulation figures high to satisfy advertisers, so broadcasters need to win audience ratings. High audience figures mean prime slots for advertisers: and prime slots can demand premium prices.

Case study – The argument against change

In 1995, a programme entitled: *J'Accuse The News* (part of Channel 4's *Without Walls* series and presented by journalist Alison Pearson) criticized developments in the presentation of broadcast news in Britain. The programme's argument was that broadcasters no longer considered the basic presentation of news in itself as being enough to prompt audiences to switch on their TV sets. And so a variety of techniques, many originating in the USA, are added to give entertainment value to news presentation. According to Pearson, broadcast news is a

> 'packaged product sold through gravitas and reliability ... a blatant branding exercise [and] a substitute for news.'

Various journalists appearing on the programme voiced their concerns that TV news in the 1990s was inhibited in its coverage of some news stories by the desire to win ratings and appease politicians; that it was sexist in its production and presentation, and biased in other areas such as sport and financial news. To Pearson, its obsession with dramatic images bordered on the 'mawkish and macabre – a technique yoked from the tabloid press.' The programme implied that investigative journalism is given a lower priority by programme makers than 'gimmickry' – state-of-the-art fancy graphics – leaving insufficient funds in the budget to pay for correspondents based worldwide.

Another accusation that the programme highlighted was that television broadcasters are reliant on the government for, in the case of the BBC, charter renewal, and in respect of ITN and the satellite companies, the licence to broadcast. Therefore television news, although not directly answerable to government, is certainly beholden to it. There is no such thing as true independence in television news, which might explain (according to the programme) why television does not scoop news items in the way that print media do, and that however honourable a journalist's intentions may be, news is always an 'edited' report of the facts.

Case study – The argument for change

Was the programme justified in all of its accusations? Is broadcast news reliant on the skills of the journalist, or the skills of the graphic artist? And is there anything that journalists can learn from these criticisms and apply to modern working methods?

In response to the programme's critique of news content, Stewart Purvis, then editor-in-chief at ITN, replied that viewers were better off because some of the in-depth items featured on programmes like *News at Ten*, were investigative and consumer reports for which there had been no previous outlet on earlier, shorter bulletins. However, since *News at Ten* was dropped from its 30-minute slot in 1999, its replacement, *ITV Nightly News*, runs at under 20 minutes with less time for the in-depth reports that Purvis cited. It could be argued that this is counterbalanced by *Tonight – with Trevor McDonald*, a weekly current affairs programme. Although occupying a 60-minute slot, its actual running time is closer to 50 owing to commercial breaks. Whether it contains greater volume of content or more time for in-depth reports than *News at Ten*, or whether this repackaging of news is more attractive to the viewer, is open to debate.

Graphics

It is unlikely that viewers in the twenty-first century would happily return to the days of newsreaders viewed in close up whilst still images 'hover' above their shoulders. Graphics enhance presentation and provide the very thing that broadcast television needs: images.

Broadcast news is now more reliant on images that at any time in its short history. Instant pictures of high quality can be edited at the location and relayed by satellite instantly and from anywhere in the world by just one person. To complement news footage, graphics can be used to examine a story in detail. The role of the graphic artist is to use computer animation to demonstrate a scenario, explain historical background, bring to life statistics or whatever the story demands. In this respect, the newsreader's role changes from being that of purely a reader. Like the viewer, the newsreader will listen while an assessed voice (expert) explains over the graphic just what is being presented and why. Graphics are also reliable aids in news presentation, with few technical failures in transmission. And because a growing percentage of the viewing population own computers – enabling them to view graphics in websites or even construct their own websites – the use of graphics in news presentation is now better understood (by the viewer).

Pictures

Because of the advances in video technology, and the increase in ownership of camcorders, members of the public are as likely to record news footage on their own cameras as a professional camera operator in certain situations. This adds to the amount of material that can be made available to broadcasters. Some enterprising individuals go out with the sole purpose of shooting news footage with camcorders made for the domestic market. For the untrained videographer hoping to capture an exclusive, the rewards can be high, with CNN particularly interested in footage of news events from around the world. However, in recent years, the goalposts have narrowed for the opportunist as editors require 'cut' footage shot on digicam and beamed without delay to the studio. Such is the pace of broadcast news.

Figure 13.1

Pictures of the starving and dying can move the viewing public into taking action, as happened in 1985 when pop stars Bob Geldof and Midge Ure committed themselves to beginning a relief campaign to help those victims of the war in Ethiopia by organizing Band Aid.

The emphasis on the dramatic picture, however, can leave the viewer bewildered and unable to keep up with the pace of events.

Presented out of context and without a full account or recap of what has caused the problem only serves to confuse. There follows a need to know how the situation progresses once the drama of the original event has passed. This is often left to documentary current affairs programmes made largely by independent production companies that cover stories with a deeper focus, working in a similar way to feature articles in newspapers. Former *Daily Mirror* journalist, John Pilger, together with producer David Munro, returned to Cambodia on no less than six occasions to film updates of the plight facing that country during the 1980s and 1990s; long after the television news crews had moved on from the story.

Culture

Criticism that television news does not cover certain countries and events, or that when it does it quickly moves on as if barely interested, is unjustified for several reasons. Some countries do not allow access to foreign news crews, and applications to enter 'friendly' countries can take months. When access is given, it can be restricted by official minders who escort the journalists everywhere. Some countries have no apparatus for disseminating news, and even if they did, there are insufficient foreign correspondents to cover every country at any one time.

That people view world events through their own cultural perspective and national interests might be considered natural, but it is also a matter for concern. As individuals, we should be able to at least try to stand aside from our own interests and biases to view a situation as neutrally as possible. The first reaction of a reporter is to talk to those who can sum up the situation clearly in general and specific terms. Often, the reporter will turn to 'experts in the field'. In developing countries, these are often aid workers who themselves might not be there had TV news not highlighted that situation.

Because of this, western audiences receive news through a western perspective of world events. The Vietnam War was a case in point. The North Vietnamese were portrayed by the western media as an enemy of democracy because they were communists backed by larger communist nations such as China and the Soviet Union –

then at loggerheads with the West. The South Vietnamese regime, on the other hand, was backed by various western powers and portrayed as democratic and capitalist. News coverage through this perspective distorted both sides of the Vietnamese story.

Interest in news stories can also fade quickly – and not necessarily public interest. Broadcast news organizations continually review their policy as to what they consider will attract viewers to news bulletins and, consequently, advertisers to the commercial slots. In 1970, American broadcast companies had already lost interest in covering what was then only the third space shot to the moon. It was only when Apollo 13 developed a technical problem, throwing the mission into jeopardy, that the shot became headline news. Today, many space shots are not considered news at all – unless something unexpected happens.

Television news is brought to our screens through a combination of variables: finance, personalities, politics, culture, history, technology. As *J'Accuse The News* made clear, there is much more to gathering the news than meets the eye.

14 | TELEVISION NEWS (2)

Reporting from ...

There can hardly be anyone under the age of 50 who has not grown up watching television news and current affairs documentaries. For many hopeful applicants to television journalism, the roles of correspondent or newsreader would seem to be the greatest career goal. And yet, if the autobiographies and interviews of those who have 'made it' are to be believed, many of the most famous faces in television news never set out to occupy such exalted positions. Indeed, during the 1950s, 1960s and much of the 1970s, television newsreaders and correspondents were not the 'star' figures their successors have since become. News bulletins were shorter, less frequent and rarely a subject for speculation by other parts of the media, which is very different from today's media interest in television news. Barely a week seems to pass when the papers do not run an article on who is doing what and how at ITN or the BBC. Even television cannot resist the opportunity to step aside from its role as news provider to promote and congratulate those who deliver the news: something that neither radio nor the print media does with their newsreaders and correspondents.

Television newsreaders and correspondents, through the amount of exposure they receive each day broadcasting, and through the interest of other parts of the media, have become celebrities. Their contracts with the companies they work for sometimes require them to fulfil roles once performed only by famous actors and entertainers: opening fêtes, giving talks and presenting prizes. They can also find themselves the subject of the news itself. Two of the more recent high-profile broadcasters to make the transition to politics include Martin Bell and Gus McDonald (now Labour Party peer, Lord McDonald). On a more tragic note, the brutal murder of

BBC newsreader and presenter Jill Dando made headline news around the world in April 1999.

The transition to celebrity status was gradual but inevitable as bulletins increased in frequency and length, colour replaced black and white, electronic news gathering (ENG) replaced film, and the desire to create new stars in the pop culture at a time when punk rock rejected and replaced the glam rock star with the anti-hero.

Back in the 1950s Robin Day made television history when he interviewed President Nasser of Egypt in 1957 using the most direct approach in his questioning that any British reporter had ever done with a politician or statesman. By today's standards, the transcript appears tame, but at that time Britain and Egypt were not on diplomatic terms over the Suez crisis. It was also one of the first occasions that a television news report made front page news headlines. This was a period when correspondents were beginning to step from out of the shadows and make a name for themselves.

Television coverage of the Vietnam War probably did more than any other event to establish the correspondent as a new kind of star or even hero in the British national psyche. Later dubbed 'the television war', Vietnam was a watershed for television news coverage of world events as correspondents and camera crews from around the world filmed daily reports of fighting. Most of these reports were of missions deep into the Vietnamese jungle and consequent 'fire fights' with an unseen enemy. This changed dramatically in 1968 with what became known as the Tet Offensive in which the Vietcong audaciously brought the fight to the Americans and their allies in the heart of the South Vietnamese capital, Saigon. In the midst of the battle, BBC correspondent Julian Pettifer was seen by millions of viewers in the UK reporting under fire and dodging bullets in the streets.

The Tet Offensive, starting as it did at the beginning of the Chinese New Year, took both the American army and foreign correspondents based in Saigon completely by surprise. What were thought initially to be the sound of firecrackers turned out to be the first shots in a daring attempt to take the city from within. Pettifer's breathless reports of the streetfighting, running with South Vietnamese soldiers, crouching with them, his eyes scanning the streets and buildings beyond the camera, did what no press article or photograph could ever do by bringing the horrifying sights and sounds of war directly into people's living rooms. Other British correspondents to make their names during the Vietnam War included Martin Bell and Keith Barron.

The correspondent was now seen as an action-hero, dressed in khaki, dodging bullets. It was a scenario that was to become more common as the last three decades of the century were played out on the world's television screens.

The role of the reporter/correspondent

Reporters and correspondents working for broadcast news-stations and agencies can be posted anywhere around the world depending on their position and the company they work for. The backgrounds they come from will often be as diverse as the news they are covering: some will have come straight from training, some will have moved to television from radio or print journalism. Many will have had early careers in non-journalistic professions, although it is not unusual for broadcast journalists to come from a career that is information or communications based, such as teaching or acting.

The difference between the terms 'reporter' and 'correspondent' refers to generalization and specialization, respectively. Whilst the reporter covers any variety of occurrences, the correspondent is regarded as a specialist on a particular subject or country.

BBC policy is to employ broadcast journalists who have completed a relevant BJTC accredited training course or from other parts of the media such as print or radio. After working in regional stations, recruitment to nationally based operations means reporting from around Britain before being sent abroad to cover international stories as correspondents.

The BBC, like other broadcasters and news agencies, selects candidates for their motivation and ability to write and understand the 'wider context' of world affairs. In addition to these abilities, Richard Sambrook, head of BBC Newsgathering, emphasizes the importance of the 'x-factor' – that all-important part of a reporter's character that is so necessary in television news. Where the radio journalist has to have good speech delivery, so the television

Figure 14.1

journalist needs a good visual delivery to convey the report. This is not about glamour but about 'presence'. Indeed, glamour would detract from the report. In theatrical or cinematic terms the x-factor would be known as star quality.

The connections between broadcast journalism and show business are many and varied. It is not unusual to find that journalists who adapt well to broadcasting have often started their careers as would-be actors. The common denominator linking the two professions is the love of communicating.

Like the actor, the reporter needs to be able to activate an internal 'switch' within the mind that enables part of the self to perform – not act, in the theatrical sense – even though in normal life they may be shy and introverted. The nearest the broadcaster comes to 'acting' is when restraining the impulse to become overly sad, angry, excited or happy in the course of a report. It is not easy to interview someone whose political ideology is the opposite to your own, and it can be very easy to lose your cool when the interviewee is postulating an opinion which is not in accordance with yours. Remember that it is not the reporter's place to take them down a peg or two. Likewise, interviewing a dictator who may be responsible for the imprisonment, torture and deaths of thousands is one of the most challenging tasks of all for the broadcast journalist – and one that is rarely granted.

Preparing to speak

The worst nightmare for all news broadcasters is the fear of realising that through the camera lens you are addressing an audience of thousands, if not millions. This is where that all-important internal switch comes into play: forget to flick it on, and disaster can strike. It is not enough to take a sip of water, clear your throat and brush the hair out of your eyes before speaking to camera. The tongue is a notorious instrument for tripping up the unprepared. This mass of muscle is rooted like a tree at its base, and like all muscles can be exercised regularly to get the best use out of it. Normally, most people do not need to exercise their tongue – unless they perform, in which case, it is a crucial activity.

Figure 14.2

Actors limber up their bodies with gentle exercises before a performance and calm the mind. This is also a good routine for broadcasters. If you are preparing to read a bulletin, or on the way to an assignment, you can do the following exercises whilst concentrating on other things.

1 Stick your tongue out and try to touch the tip of your nose with it.
2 Without drawing the tongue in, aim to lick in one sweep across your top lip, cheek, bottom lip, cheek and back to the tip of your nose (or near enough).

3 Repeat and then change direction

Hurts, doesn't it? There are less painful ways of exercising the tongue, although these should be used in conjunction with the above exercise. Now, ...

4 Blow raspberries (rude but effective).
5 Wag the tongue up and down (slowly) keeping it as far out of your mouth as possible.

Saying tongue-twisters is also a good way of getting your tongue to do what you want it to do. The following tongue-twister is one commonly used by actors before going on stage:

The tip of the tongue taking a trip of three steps down the palette to tap at three on the teeth.

If you say it properly, taking care to enunciate and exaggerate every syllable, it will take the tongue through all the various movements normally encountered in English speech. Other old favourites are:

Peter Piper picked a peck of pickled peppers.

The rain in Spain falls mainly on the plain.

Enunciate with care; this latter phrase only worked for Eliza Doolittle after much practice and great deliberation.

Here's the most simple of all:

Butter-gutter

Too simple? Repeat it continuously and speed it up. Go as fast as you can without turning it into 'Budder-gudder'.

The good thing with exercising the tongue is that exercise not only loosens the tongue, making it easier to enunciate, but also improves confidence.

It is also a good idea to exercise the voice, though you will not need to project in the same way as the actor or singer. The following exercise is easily done. It works best if you are lying on your back but can be done from a sitting position using good posture, or standing. Like the tongue exercise, try getting into the habit of doing it regularly and find somewhere quiet and private that also allows you the chance to relax a little. However, do not be self-conscious about these exercises: it is your job to communicate to the best of your ability. This exercise is particularly good for helping you broadcast your delivery at an even pitch and pace.

1 Inhale, then let the breath out on a word ('mah' or 'moo' are words that flow easily) in a controlled manner keeping pitch and volume constant.

2 Imagine that you can see the word stretching out in front of you further and further.

3 You don't need to be loud, soft is good – simply maintain pitch and volume.

4 Use your diaphragm to keep control and keep going until you run out of breath.

5 Take another breath, alter the key and use a different monosyllabic word.

Learn to be your own critic. If you can, stand mentally aside from yourself: watch and listen to your performance. If you are playing an active part in editing your material, you will be forced to observe your 'performance' many times over. Do not concern yourself with the nuances of small mannerisms; these will add to your credibility rather than detract, provided you are not faking mannerisms in order to adopt a persona. Always be yourself. Never try to mimic anyone else.

Planning

The scout's motto, 'Be prepared', should also be the reporter's. There is no better advice that can be given. By the time you've reached that sought-after position of television news reporter, you will already be an experienced journalist who knows much about the process of finding and reporting stories. As before, your editor will brief you and you will research the story and prepare accordingly. But the chances are that you may never have worked quite like this before.

All television news companies vary their policy regarding how reporters and correspondents operate in the field. Some reporters get more help than others, but generally the reporter is self-sufficient, relying on personal experience and much tenacity to get them through an assignment.

Figure 14.3

Get into the habit of keeping two travel bags packed. Their contents should include:

- appropriate changes of clothes for warm and cold climates
- world map showing time zones
- Swiss Army knife
- alarm clock
- toiletries
- first-aid kit
- various bathroom plugs or a fit-all size
- compass
- shoe shine kit/travel iron
- short-wave radio (for listening to BBC World Service and Voice of America)
- electric appliance adapter
- small tape recorder or mini-disc
- compact camera
- small torch
- cash in US dollars (correspondents abroad find that dollars are accepted as currency in many countries).

Keep two full passports so that you have the appropriate visas stamped and ready. Although some countries will stamp visas on entry, others are best applied for at home. At least with two, you will always have one passport ready to go.

Make sure that you are up to date with inoculations and keep a record of them as part of your passport. Ideally, you should be inoculated against typhoid, meningitis, cholera, yellow fever and tetanus. Malaria can only be counteracted by taking tablets before and after your visit. It also pays to keep well covered in countries where the mosquito that carries malaria is active. Advice can be sought from your GP or from British Airways which runs travel clinics in some of the larger cities. Even if you're working in another EU country, you should obtain form E111 from your local post office: this enables you to receive emergency medical treatment should you need it in a member country.

If, in your first-aid kit, you intend to carry syringes and needles, be sure to declare these on arrival in countries as you may be suspected of being a drug addict.

In respect of driving abroad, carry an international driver's permit (IDP). In some countries, if police or soldiers stop you and ask to see your driving licence, offer the IDP first as they might retain it, leaving you free to continue using your main national licence.

When the call comes to go, know how to use the Internet to find some basic information about the place you are travelling to. Do not waste time checking out various search engines; you should already be sure of a good one, so stick to it. In addition to websites, your office may well have archive files with either general or specific information relating to your assignment. Know whether it is your responsibility to book the flight or hire a car. Make sure you know how the system works from day one in the job; it is no good complaining later. If the assignment is abroad, buy a travel guide for the place you are going to. Working abroad, the need to familiarize yourself with the country's etiquette is particularly important. A basic knowledge of etiquette will make your job abroad much easier and can also win you friends – which is important if you are to work effectively as a reporter.

In the field

Whether you are reporting from outside the local law court within minutes of your studio base, or from a war zone on the other side of the world, the way you work in a team is crucial. In fact, the team normally consists of just two people – you, as reporter/correspondent, and the camera operator.

In regional newsrooms, camera operators are often freelance 'stringers' on call to cover stories within a particular area. They bring their own cameras and ancillary equipment. Their role complements that of the salaried camera crews.

When abroad, reporters may find themselves working with camera crews from a national station or even with another international crew. It all depends on the situation – and no two situations are ever the same.

Over the years, good friendships can be established and it is not unusual to see the same old faces turning up to cover stories. Although rivals in one respect, there is a common background and a shared objective between reporters and camera operators where good working relationships and friendships are formed.

The 'old hands' – reporters and camera operators with established reputations – will always readily help newcomers. Their knowledge and experience are invaluable. Different crews work in different ways; each time you work with a new camera operator the effort to bond as a team begins over again, but each time it is worth the effort. The happier both of you are with one another, the greater the results.

As a newcomer, you will not be wrong in assuming that your camera operator will be considerably more experienced than you. Never consider yourself to be a 'rank' above – you are not. You both have very different but equally important roles to perform and will be relying on one another completely. A good icebreaker on first meeting is to proffer a bar of chocolate or sweets (not mints as your new colleague might think you are hinting at bad breath). Offer to carry some of the heavy or bulky equipment such as the 'legs' (tripod) – and not just once but every time, so that a working pattern between you starts to establish itself. Do not try to carry the camera unless asked to do so, as most operators guard this precious item with their lives.

By all means confer over the set-up of a shot, but be prepared to defer to experience in many cases. A good camera operator should explain why certain shots work and others do not. Refrain from peering down the camera viewfinder each time a shot is set-up as if you were the director. In time, that role may become your responsibility, but for now concentrate on the job in hand. If you are invited to check the shot, fair enough.

Setting up a shot is not always as straightforward as it may appear to be. Some shots have become clichéd in television history: the pictures of the political correspondent in front of Number 10, Downing Street, or Washington's Capitol building; Scotland Yard with its revolving reflective sign. The inclusion of symbols that will signify a location are the most obvious. If it is a piece about the theatre on Broadway for British audiences, the reporter does not set up a shot stood in front of the Statue of Liberty just because the statue also signifies New York and the USA in particular. The subject of the piece may be about one particular theatre; if so, set up the camera in front of that theatre; if it is a general piece about the Broadway theatre in general, then set up the shot to show as much of Broadway as possible and one that is also recognizable to those who have visited the area or through having seen it before in other reports. In this respect, it becomes clichéd but it also succeeds in conveying the scene.

Before the camera rolls, do not be afraid to ask for a second opinion on your appearance. Even using a mirror, you may not have spotted something slightly askew. For those who have been in the armed forces or enjoy sub-aqua diving, it is normal to have your friend help you adjust the gear you are wearing. This is part of what is known as the buddy system and it is a good habit to get into when working in the field. Adopt the buddy system and look out for one another. One day, not only your reputation, but your lives may depend on it.

Some set-ups ask for trouble. For example, trying to shoot a piece to camera about soccer fan clubs whilst standing in the midst of soccer supporters making their way into or out of the stadium is not recommended. Happy supporters on the way in often delight in showing off in front of a camera by pulling faces and playfully jostling the reporter. On the way out, the mood might be ugly. If possible, set up a distance from the main throng so that the supporters can be seen in the background but are not close enough to interfere with the shot, or try to find an elevated position that overlooks the supporters.

Be careful, also, to avoid reflections from large panes of glass such as shop windows. These can reflect all sorts of things from other camera crews to members of the public standing to watch, all of which create distractions for the viewer.

Reporters familiar with reporting for radio news will not need to be told about the importance of sound – especially too much sound. Microphones have become very sophisticated, but do not put yourself in a position where you cannot hear yourself speak. Usually, reports can be made from busy motorways, airports or crowded streets without problem. The one that catches most reporters out is the unexpected noise – sometimes deliberate. This might be as innocuous as a church bell, a generator starting up or the blasting of a ship's horn in the docks. As a rule, if it runs, moves or ticks, beware.

Remaining detached is one of the hardest parts of being a reporter. There may be times when you will report from a war zone or former war zone where famine is rife and the orphanages full. Refrain from offering those things you cannot sustain. It is a natural human feeling to want to go to the car and bring out your sandwiches to give to those that are starving, or hand out sweets to orphans. On no account must you ever do this. To offer one person a sandwich or a child a sweet under such conditions can cause a riot as desperate people scramble for what few meagre items you offer. In the mêlée, people get hurt and will not be able to understand why you cannot offer more. This is in addition to fragile digestive systems that will not be able to cope. Do your job to transmit the awful scene to the world, but let the aid organizations do what they do best.

Monologues

Monologues to camera are difficult at the beginning of a reporter's career but get easier with time. That said, time is not on the side of the reporter. It is convention to look directly into the camera lens, not to read from a notebook, although a notebook or clipboard can be referred to when quoting details such as a judge's summing-up. As with the warm-up exercises for the tongue and voice, there are methods from the theatre that can be used to help you learn the lines you have written. In order to use this method to your advantage, think about the intention of what you are trying to say rather than the words. Consider describing the story in a variety of terms rather than specific words. You might write this:

Example

The fifteenth-century church of St Dunstan's narrowly escaped bombing in 1941 to become a focal point for the local community who used the building as a meeting room when the town hall was destroyed and as a temporary shelter for those made homeless during the blitz. Since then it has seen a steady decline in worshippers.

However, moves by the church authorities to sell off the building and its adjacent land including the cemetery have met with stiff opposition from locals who feel it is part of the community's history. Legend has it that King Charles the First prayed in the church during the Civil War and that Dick Turpin actually spent a night sleeping on one of the pews.

If the authorities get their way, this will be the fiftieth parish church sold for private development in the last five years. Opposing the sell off, former councillor Rose Mitward-Zellor is spearheading an action group dedicated to preserving the church, which it is felt is worthy of special preservation having survived against the odds when so much of this part of the city was devastated: first by bombing and later by V1 and V2 rocket attacks.

Although the bishop of Medgate, in whose diocese the church stands, was unable to comment today, both the church authorities and parish council confirm that a preservation order prevents the church from being demolished. This hasn't appeased locals who are making it clear that they want the church to remain a working part of their community.

Sandy Beach, for TKN News at Nine.

To attempt to remember this report verbatim would be difficult, worrying and time consuming. And the more you worry about being word perfect, the more difficult it becomes to deliver the piece to camera. Writing the piece clarifies the information in your mind, helping you to put all the pieces into perspective and time it, but that does not mean that what you have written should be what you say to camera.

Keeping the narrative order, consider the main points of the report: medieval church up for sale; local people want to save it. Think about people's aims: the church wants to sell; the community want to save.

Think about objectives: the church authorities no longer need it because of falling attendance; the community want it because it is still a focal point which is important to them. What about facts and figures? These are always difficult to remember. You can always substitute fifteenth century with late medieval: 1941 with Second World War. And if you need to, attach a note to the tripod legs in bold letters saying: 50th church, Charles 1, Dick Turpin, V1, V2, in that order.

Now simplify it by telling the story from memory as if you were recounting it to a friend. It may sound something like this:

'You know that late medieval church of St Dunstan's, the one that narrowly escaped bombing in the Second World War to become a focal point for locals? They used it as a meeting room and shelter for those made homeless by the bombing. Well, ever since then the number of people going to church has dropped. Anyway, the authorities want to sell the building and cemetery. This hasn't gone down well with the locals who say it's part of their history. Apparently, King

Charles the First prayed in the church during the Civil War and Dick Turpin even spent a night on a pew.

If the authorities get their way, this will be the fiftieth church sold in five years. But the community's fighting back with an action group. They say it's special because of its history and surviving the bombing – V2 rockets, everything.

The bishop of Medgate hasn't said anything, but the authorities and parish council have said that a preservation order means the church won't be pulled down. Mind you, the locals still aren't happy; they're insisting that it stays part of the community.'

Once you realize that you can remember the basics, the rest becomes easier as your confidence grows. We all tell similar accounts to our friends and family on a regular basis using a natural capacity to remember facts and figures without giving it a second thought. What makes presenting a piece to camera difficult is the formal presentation of facts and figures. Reporters are expected to be conventional and to talk in a style that is economical and formal. Like the news writer, the reporter cannot indulge in clichés, redundant phrases or repeat the point. The constraint is not space, but time.

Although initially difficult, these monologues become easier as the brain's capacity to memorize large amounts of text increases. There are other methods to make monologues easier, but try to avoid the easy options such as recording the piece to a small tape recorder or mini-disc and playing it back through an earphone as an audible cue. Not only can this system fail at the worst moment, it does not help you to memorize and you end up becoming reliant on a tool that you may one day lose or forget to buy batteries for.

Interviews

Interviewing for reporters in the field can take the shape of a recorded interview in which the interviewee addresses a question from the reporter who is out of vision. In transmission, the cue for this is a voice-over: 'I asked the minister whether she would be standing in the next election.' The picture that follows is of the minister replying to the question and probably addressing a group of journalists. Similar footage and even the same answer might be seen on another channel's news programme.

The other type of interview, known as down-the-line, is a live piece transmitted direct to the studio. Here, once the opening question is put, the camera will focus on the interviewee and pull out at the end of the interview to include the reporter in vision. The reporter thanks the interviewee, turns to camera and hands back to the studio.

For those reporters with a background in radio journalism, broadcast interview techniques will have been honed over time: thinking ahead, mentally editing, listening and nodding attentively, and never letting the gaze wander when listening, as if something else were more important.

The most important consideration for the reporter when first approaching a possible interviewee is whether the interview is genuinely going to propel the narrative of the story and whether the person concerned is truly a part of that story or merely a bystander. You should be sure of the line of questioning that your interview is going to take. Do not ask them what they want to be asked: you are not there to promote them. Do you intend to discover something new through the interview? Or is it just an exercise to fill out the report with sound bites and footage because you could not get the person you really wanted?

It is a good idea, too, to write in note form the interviewee's name and title, such as Lieutenant Colonel Harry Saunders-Mitchum-Kales of the fifth battalion Light Infantry, or whatever. And make sure you know how your interviewee wants to be addressed. For example, the commissioned army rank of Lieutenant Colonel should not be confused with other commissioned ranks such as Lieutenant or Colonel.

Some of the most difficult interviews are those in which you find yourself in a scrum with other reporters from print and radio. Be prepared to feel a hand on your shoulder pulling you to one side, or a voice telling you to 'get out the way!' If you have never had experience of this feeding frenzy as it is sometimes called, do not be put off. Whatever your size, stand your ground and concentrate on the job in hand.

News conferences are more civilized affairs and run on official guidelines as either a regular occurrence or arranged in advance by the organizers. Owing to the large number of press reporters who will turn up, it can be difficult to put a question forward and also intimidating for the newcomer. Like the scrum, do not be put off, and remember that you are a journalist like everyone else. Take note of the questions your colleagues ask so as not to repeat them. Sometimes, the questions put by others will cover the things you may want to ask, but if you have a leading question that no one else has thought of, don't hesitate – ask.

Phrasing questions is another difficult aspect of television interviewing. If the questions are too long and rambling, they can be misinterpreted accidently or deliberately by the interviewee, depending on their experience in front of the cameras. Too polite, and you give the impression of being apologetic for asking or just grateful for whatever response you can get. Nor should you bluff as it is likely to catch you out. When interviewers have referred to an oblique source such as: 'It's rumoured that you've been seen with', or 'Sources say that you've been seen with', it encourages the response: 'What rumours? What sources? Name them.' If a document, which might be a press release or published newspaper, cites something concerning your line of questioning to the interviewee, then use it if is legally possible to do so: 'The *Daily Blah* states that you've been seen with ... Is it true or not?' By doing so, you are referring to the newspaper report, not rumour that you cannot substantiate.

Be specific in the way you phrase questions, and ask pertinent questions with conviction. This is an acquired skill and one that will win you respect from viewers, editors and interviewees. Remember that it is not your job as interviewer to psychoanalyse, debate with, prosecute or promote the interviewee.

Listening and allowing the interviewee to answer in full is another skill acquired over time. Some reporters seem to think that the more questions they can ask in an interview, the more it will appear that they are doing their job correctly and getting results. Added to this is the pressure to get a package back to the studio. Either of these can result in a hurried interview where the main points are lost.

Where possible, allow good time for the interview. Politicians, particularly when they are in power, are well known for avoiding questions and steering the interview onto their own agenda. It is the job of the interviewer to get it back on course – but you should pay particular attention to what the politician is saying as there may be something that can be picked up on. When you want interviewees to speak openly, allow them time to collect their thoughts. A refugee may have more to say to a reporter who encourages them to talk openly of their experiences without time constraint. To interrupt at times like this would be to miss much of what was being conveyed.

Packages

A package is a picture report and much more complex to produce than a piece to camera. Typically, it will be a montage of footage with voice-over and sometimes a piece to camera as well. It is a detailed report of a current news story. For example, the piece about the St Dunstan's church sell-off could be used to run with a story about the annual meeting of the Church Synod where the ethics of church closures are being debated.

In constructing a package, the reporter needs to have good visualization. It is not enough simply to shoot a few minutes of the church inside and out and expect the commentary to fit flawlessly on top of pictures of granite and gravestones. The reporter needs to talk to those people involved with the church and particularly its preservation, such as the leader of the action group, Rose Mitward-Zellor. Interviews also need to be in context; there is no point in talking to the action group leader in a setting unrelated to the church she's dedicated to saving. It is imperative when planning to arrange interviews at the church and, if possible, at an action group meeting.

Through research you will be able to put together an outline treatment on paper (see Figure 14.4). The treatment provides the opportunity to write down your ideas about pictures and sound. This is where visualization is important. List the shots you think will be most important on the left and sound/commentary on the right. Use pencil as you will want to erase some items as new ideas come to you. To estimate time, you can use two methods:

Picture

1. Ext. Church
Poss. Archive footage blitz, V2
rockets,

> Exterior shot

> Voice-over

Sound
V/O Commentary: The fifteenth-
century church of St Dunstan's -
steady decline in worshippers.

> You can add commentary
> later – after the interview

> Check with newsroom
> whether archive film available

2. Ext. church me walking
past graves

> Long shot

To camera: (L.S.) However,
moves by the church - it is
part of the community's history

Poss. stills - Charles I,
Dick Turpin

Legend has it - sleeping on one
of the pews

> Interior shot

3. Int. Action group meeting

If the authorities get their way
- later by V1 and V2 rocket
attacks

4. Int. Interview: Rose
Mitward-Zellor

Tell me how you intend to
save the church from closure?

5. Int. Church, RM-Z working in
church (if poss.)
Or Ext. RM-Z walking in grounds
talking to me

> Be flexible with
> ideas for shots

6. To camera - summing up

Although the bishop of Medgate
- a working part of their community

Figure 14.4   How your treatment might look

1 Three words equal one second is pretty accurate, but it means a lot of calculation counting words and multiplying by three.

2 Alternatively, for each point you make, allow 15 seconds (you will not be far out): two points in your commentary = 30 seconds, and so on: 'The fifteenth-century church of St Dunstan's narrowly escaped bombing – Since then it has seen a steady decline in worshippers.' (15 seconds)

When you meet with the camera operator, you will be able to confer using the treatment as a guide. If the weather is good when you arrive at the location, the exterior shots can be done, leaving the interiors to later. Reverse this if the weather is bad. Alternatively, permission may have been refused for you to enter the church, so use the treatment to sketch a contingency plan. Remember, treatments should not be carved in stone.

Whilst the camera operator shoots exterior and interior shots of the church, you can record the interview on an audio recorder. The interview will need to be edited to time. Packages are normally of three or four minutes duration so an interview needs to be well within that and to fit in with the voice-over. Here, the ability to spot extraneous parts of the interview without losing the essential elements of the argument is vital.

With the camera operator, you will shoot an interview against a background relevant to the story (perhaps outside the church) and it is a good idea to shoot some footage of the interviewee doing something other than the interview. In this case, they might have functions to perform in the church – polishing brass, for example. This gives the viewer an insight into the role the interviewee has in preserving the church. The shot should have a different background from that of the interview and show the interviewee leaving the picture, otherwise you will have a 'jump cut'. This footage may not be used in the final cut, but for the sake of a few minutes shooting it is worth having.

For the purposes of continuity, you will need to get from your interviewee self-contained answers that do not start with yes or no. One method is to prefix the question with either who, what, where, when, which, why, or how. The other is to encourage the interviewee to talk about the situation: 'Tell me how you intend to save the church from closure.'

Once the interview is complete, you can write up the commentary – part of which can be used as a piece to camera that will run at the end of the package. As reporter, you also need to be aware of what footage has been shot so that a shot-list can be compiled. Without knowing in what order the shots should run, you would have to resort to guesswork and hope that words fit pictures.

It is important, too, that you write commentary that takes into account the day's changing events. Although the bishop of Medgate has so far refused to comment, he may well comment at the Church Synod whilst the package is being put together. It would look ridiculous if, in the commentary, he is reported as not commenting when later in the day, he does.

Time each sequence carefully and provide the editor at the studio with cues and suggestions included on the tape:

> *'The interview with Rose Mitward-Zellor begins in three seconds from now ...(pause).'*

In creating a package, you are working as researcher, director, interviewer, writer, editor and producer so that a finished package can be delivered or transmitted directly to base. The package is very much the reporter's creation. Working with a capable camera operator who will shoot comprehensive footage from varying angles, a package can be put together in a matter of hours. Once it is complete, you will need to talk by phone to the editor and studio writer to check that everything is all right and explain anything that may not be clear. This is followed by a call to the assignments desk to confirm the job is done.

When putting together a package, the reporter needs to be mindful of the following factors:

- Don't over-run the length of the piece.
- Adjust the commentary to fit the pictures.
- Note shots on a shot-list in sequential order.
- Provide cues for the editor and studio writer (who might also be the newsreader).

■ Information should not be out of date in respect of the day's events.

■ Leave the newsreader enough material with which to introduce the piece.

Newsreader   At the Church's Annual General Synod today, there has been much debate over the policy of selling off parish churches where congregation attendance figures have fallen dramatically. Debate on the subject hasn't been confined to the Synod. Residents of one parish in South London have formed an action group to save one of the city's most historic churches. Our religious affairs reporter, Sandy Beach, has been to the parish of Chadney to investigate.

Reporter   The fifteenth-century church of St Dunstan's narrowly escaped bombing in 1941 ...

By leaving enough material to provide an introduction for the newsreader, nothing is repeated.

As the compilation of packages becomes routine for the reporter, the quicker and easier they are to produce. It helps to have knowledge of how news is written and edited in the newsroom and of camera techniques and television news conventions.

For the contact book

The Royal Television Society
Holborn Hall
100 Grays Inn Road
London WC1X 8AL
Tel: 020 7430 1000
Fax: 020 7430 0924
E-mail: info@rts.org.uk
Internet: www.rts.org.uk

Training

BBC Training and Development:
The Bristol News Training Centre
Broadcasting House
Whiteladies Road
Bristol BS8 2LR

Currently, only BBC staff are trained at the News Training Centre, though this might change in the future.

For advice on training courses contact:

Broadcast Journalism Training Council
39 Westbourne Gardens
London W2 5NR
Tel: 020 7727 9522
Fax: 020 7727 9522
E-mail: secretary@bjtc.org.uk

Books

Harris Watts, *On Camera. How to Produce Film and Video*. BBC Books, 1990
Contents include: research; reconnaissance; location shooting; interviews; statements to camera; dubbing commentary; and much more.

Ted White, *Broadcast News, Reporting and Production* (2nd edition). Focal Press, 1996
Contents include: broadcast news writing; the book 'examines the skills, techniques and challenges of writing and reporting for broadcast'.

Ivor Yorke, *Television News* (3rd edition). Focal Press, 2000
Contents include: getting into television; who does what in television news; writing to pictures; reporting techniques; constructing a news programme; presenting the news; and much more.

Ivor Yorke, *Basic TV Reporting*. Focal Press, 1997
Contents include: writing techniques; reporting skills; the reporter as producer; covering news items; and much more.

15 | RADIO JOURNALISM

Radio has a very defined set of responsibilities simply because it is relaying a 'picture' that no one can see. This seems obvious, but many people involved in radio production are prone to forget it. Radio broadcasts can seem deceptively easy, perhaps because there aren't any pictures to reveal what is going on. Nothing is immortalized – as it is in print – to condemn the author. What is spoken incorrectly can be quickly glossed over as the words fade into the ether. It is the fear of 'dead air' (silence) that seems to concern radio people most of all. This is a similar concern to the one newspaper people have with blank spaces on a page or that TV people have when there are no pictures. This concern can lead to obsession that becomes all-consuming – and which should be fought.

Radio is sometimes criticized by those who feel that it is too preoccupied with filling dead air: with producing programmes that all sound the same, hosted by interchangeable presenters who seem unable to project individuality. Far from producing 'stars', radio produces a succession of soundalike clones speaking a colloquial tongue that has its roots in the Britain of the late 1960s. Radio can seem loath to change and clings to the idea that it is broadcasting to a multitude of other 'clones' rather than to a multitude of individuals. For too long, it seems to have been content to provide a training ground for journalists, presenters and producers who have their sights set on television as the ultimate career goal. Unfortunately, it also seems to be considered the poor relation.

This chapter looks at the mechanics of radio journalism from recording vox pops to reading the news. We might call it the essential mechanics of broadcast journalism. But what cannot be included in this chapter – because it cannot be taught – is that special component within you that recognizes what broadcast journalism should be and can be.

Different stations

In the UK, there are four distinct types of radio broadcaster licensed to broadcast music and speech-based programming within territorial waters: BBC, national commercial radio, independent local radio and community radio.

The BBC owns and operates 39 non-commercial stations, funded by payments drawn from the television licence and transmitting a variety of programmes on FM and medium wave. Daily programme content is a rich mix of topics from local news and features to entertainment. There is a strong element of local participation, with listeners calling in to speak on air. Local news is gathered and presented by staff journalists who prepare and read bulletins at hourly intervals. Bulletins include national and local news. The Corporation's policy of bi-media production and newsgathering means that both local radio and regional BBC TV stations can share resources where it is necessary to do so. This means that reporters from both TV and radio could be asked to compile a report for broadcast on either medium.

National commercial radio licences have been awarded to three stations, each contrasting with the other in output and each presenting its own news bulletins. They are Classic FM, Talk Radio UK and Virgin Radio.

Transmitting on the FM wavelength, independent local radio (ILR) is made up of independent commercial companies that make their money from advertising revenue. They apply to the Independent Broadcasting Authority (IBA) for their licence to broadcast. Generally, there are fewer opportunities for journalists at the various local stations although Independent Radio News (IRN), which supplies news for the various independents, employs journalists.

In addition to the main three, there is community radio – local stations with a licence to broadcast non-commercially as non-profit-making ventures manned by volunteers. Community radio was established chiefly to work in hospitals where volunteers visit patients to talk and take requests for records that can be played back at the studio and piped to headphones placed at the hospital bed. For those wanting to work in radio, community or hospital radio provides the first open door. It is invaluable for the experience it gives in talking to people, using a music library, producing and presenting.

Case study

Britain might never have seen the growth of BBC local stations or the arrival of independent radio had it not been for the pioneering work of the 'pirate' radio stations. Steaming just beyond British territorial waters and operating from converted lighthouse ships and small freighters, the aptly named pirates were funded as private enterprises. Their objective was to transmit (and promote) the burgeoning rock and pop sounds of the 1960s for which the BBC, before 1967, did not cater. Mention should also be made of an independent station also beyond territorial waters that was not so much a pirate but a well-established 'British' broadcasting institution by the 1960s: Radio Luxembourg. This was a British-run radio station transmitting from the Grand Duchy of Luxembourg to the UK and the Continent and had been doing so for over 30 years when the pop revolution of the 1960s happened. The only drawback to Radio Luxembourg and the pirates was that listeners had to wait until after dark before tuning in for a near decent reception as frequency levels only improved during the hours of darkness.

By the late 1980s, Radio Luxembourg and the pirates had all but disappeared from the airwaves. The historic role they played in creating the diverse range of British radio stations that we now have, and importantly the promotion of British popular music and culture, is beyond measure. Mention should also be made of the many radio careers it launched and the creation of styles in presentation and working practices still in use. Historically, the period is worth careful study for anyone wishing to work in radio today.

Pirate stations continue to operate in some parts of Britain and are based largely in the cities rather than at sea or abroad.

Today's pirates are as original as their predecessors were in their output, transmitting specifically to audiences who feel their tastes are not catered for on mainstream radio. Some of them eventually gain a licence to broadcast, one of the more recent being Kiss FM.

Graduates in broadcast radio journalism can apply for their first jobs to BBC local radio – with its speech-based programming – or to an ILR station with its largely music-based programming. Despite applying for a job described as, say, reporter, the chances are that, as a newcomer, you will be expected to perform a wide range of tasks that include writing and presenting news bulletins, manning the phones, standing in for the receptionist, scanning the local newspapers and maybe even presenting a show. It is a very challenging area of journalism and one that is more suited to the technically minded than the technophobe.

Reporting

The responsibility for finding news stories falls on the shoulders of all reporters, however new they may be to the station or industry in general. Sometimes it presents itself with public relations companies and press officers faxing through developments at the council, local college or police station, but generally the job of finding news remains a 24-hour watch.

Like the newspaper reporter, the radio reporter needs to cultivate contacts in the local community – who, after all, are the target audience. Although you may be looking towards local press for news and inspiration, ironically, they will be watching (or rather listening) to you – and often radio does scoop everyone when it comes to finding the stories. This is simply because news is broadcast on radio at least every hour – something newspapers cannot match. It is important, of course, to update that news constantly, so that the 10 am bulletin is carrying updated information on breaking stories that the 9 am bulletin covered, and so on.

The need to know what the listeners want to hear by way of news is crucial. For example, in a rural area that is heavily dependent on agriculture, farming news will obviously have a high priority. But it is not simply the category that makes a story important; it is the basic ingredients.

In Britain, national radio news works to a different set of priorities from that of local. The local news can personalize its coverage by getting the reaction of those directly affected in the community. Suppose there has been an unexpectedly heavy snowstorm covering the south-west of England in April causing farmers on the Mendip hills to lose hundreds of newborn lambs. Reporters talk to a Mendip farmer about the problems he is having. When this is reported on national news, the reaction of many viewers might be to switch off because they cannot identify with what has happened. Their region might be experiencing warm sunshine or rain; they might live in the middle of a big city; perhaps they cannot understand what the farmer is saying because of his Somerset accent. For a local audience, though, the late snow and the farmer's struggle to rescue his flock is big news. A few hundred people may well know the farmer personally and the immediate area in which he lives. They might identify with him and may even offer to help in some respect. This is where local news comes into its own: it helps to unify a community throughout the year.

It does help to have some specialist knowledge of the community that you are working in. The first thing you need to realize is that wherever you work and report from, people are generally proud of their community and identity. It may be that the seats in the town park were vandalized two years ago and still have not been replaced, or that the streets are littered and nobody seems to care. This does not mean that local pride isn't there – most often, it is. Older people may talk of better days they knew in the past, and hope that better days are to come. This in itself is news, especially if concerted efforts are being made to restore local amenities. All counties have tremendous pride in their histories and celebrate their individuality; it is worth remembering this at all times.

A few trips to the local library and county museum will help you to identify the unique position the county or region has played in the nation's history. Spending time and effort to do this homework will pay dividends. Take special care in getting to know local place names so that you pronounce them correctly.

Actuality

Because radio is dependent on sound and the spoken word, the need to have actuality when reporting news is important. Where possible, the radio reporter needs to be at the scene to report directly on what is happening or what has happened. If this is not possible, the reporter can talk to people over the telephone from the studio in order to get a 'soundbite' – but it must be from people who are in some way involved in the story. They may be a local government officer talking about a political decision of local interest; an eye-witness to an accident; a witness who arrived at the scene later, but can give an 'official view' – usually a police officer or firefighter; and finally, the 'expert', or 'assessed voice' – called in to interpret a situation or incident.

Handling the equipment

Mini-disc (MD) recorders and audio software computer programs have largely replaced the use of tape machines for recording stories and editing, although you may still come across tape machines at some stations. It pays to familiarize yourself with both systems.

Figure 15.1

Microphones continue to improve in technical quality. Consider the microphone as an ear for the recorder and especially as an ear for the listener. There are two distinct types of microphone that you will come across: an omni-directional and a uni-directional. The uni-directional necessitates your tilting the microphone towards the subject when they speak and back towards you when you speak. If your sound levels are adjusted correctly, you should not have to push it right under their chin. The uni-directional microphone picks up sounds from directly in front (the subject) and behind (you) and cleverly ignores sounds coming from either side. (If you could see the two fields of sound, they would form a figure of eight.) Omni-directional microphones pick up sound from all around, in a circular pattern, and require little directional movement. These are not so good if you are trying to talk to one person in a crowd, as omnis will pick up all the noises around you.

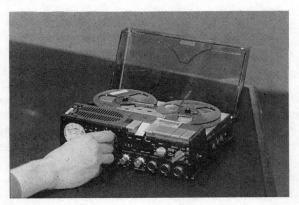

Figure 15.2

When holding a microphone, always loop the excess cable around your hand so as to reduce what is known as mic rattle. This interference sounds like a baby's rattle being shaken when you play back the recording. Before you begin recording a person's voice, you will need to get a sound level. This is important as recorders can be adjusted for levels of sound, and people's voices can vary in strength. A good method is to ask them to say their full name (and to spell it), and their title or profession. You will need this information when writing a cue. Any sentence they utter will do, just as long as they speak naturally and you can see that the recording level indicated by a needle is not going too far into the red zone of the volume unit (VU) gauge. If it does, adjust the recording level. Mini-discs do this automatically.

Figure 15.3

Also, record some atmosphere – this is background sound and might be anything from the gentle noises heard in an average sitting room to the industrial sounds of a factory or shipyard. About 20 or 30 seconds is enough and you can use it to set the scene of your story by placing it at the head or tail of your edit or on a second soundtrack.

You may need to point the microphone slightly towards the subject when they speak and back towards you when you speak, depending on the distance between you and other sounds around you. Unless you and your subject differ greatly in height, hold the microphone so that it feels comfortable and is not obtrusive to your interviewee. If you have to stick it under their chin to get a sound, then something is wrong. Before recording, make sure that there will not be any sudden sounds to interrupt the recording, such as a telephone ringing, a fridge motor cutting in or a clock chiming. If there is any likelihood of an unexpected noise, ask if the apparatus can be switched off or conduct the interview somewhere else.

To improve the quality of recorded sounds, microphones are normally fitted with a 'wind screen'. This is a spherical foam cone placed over the recording end. As its name suggests, it reduces wind noise.

Whether you are using a tape recorder or a mini-disc, always make sure that you have spare batteries with you and enough space on the tape or disc to record your piece – you would be surprised at the number of radio journalists who get caught out.

Interviews

If radio news simply revolved around a newsreader speaking reports it would be boring and lack credibility. The listener would have only the newsreader's version of events. So, including in a bulletin the voices of people making the news helps to relay a greater picture to the listener. These soundbites are as important to radio as pictures are to television news.

An interview explains and expands upon a story. The reporter speaks directly to those involved in order to convey feeling and atmosphere. This can capture the anger and frustration of a householder whose home has been flooded after heavy rains, or the joy of parents when their child makes a full recovery in hospital. The interview is not just good news for the radio station, it also provides a mouthpiece for the person in the news and, if properly edited, puts their argument in context and gives the story greater balance. More about this later in the section on editing.

How do you look?

There is a great temptation when working in radio to go about your duties casually dressed. As a journalist, you may see presenters turning up to do a show wearing jeans and a sweatshirt. This is fine for the studio but no good for the journalist who is out and about meeting people. If you do not dress seriously, how can you expect anyone to take you seriously? When you watch television news, you do not see the newsreader or correspondent dressed in casual clothes, so do likewise. Journalists are smart people and journalism is a smart profession to be in.

There is another reason behind a smart appearance: amongst communities, radio journalists are often regarded as stars. Being heard across the region has its glamorous side, and you achieve a certain amount of fame for doing it. Once you have been with a station for some time, you might start getting fan mail and some people might even recognize your voice when you go into a shop to buy something. Don't let your listeners, your station or yourself down by being scruffy.

Personality interviews

Interviewing famous people can be daunting, not necessarily because of anything they may do or say to unnerve you, but because you realize that you are talking to someone who has considerable success in their field and is held in high esteem.

As with all interviews, brief yourself on the subject's background. If the person is very famous and well established, the chances are there will be a book or two on them in the local library. If the personality is in town to promote their show at the local theatre or their new book, find out as much information as you can about this latest venture. Nothing irritates an interviewee more than a journalist or presenter who has not done their research. To ask a famous author, 'What brings you here, to Townchester?' when it is blatantly obvious that they are in town to promote their latest book, deserves the contempt it will undoubtedly receive.

In many cases, personalities only agree to interviews on the strength of promoting their latest venture. However, do not interview simply to allow them to plug. The listener will want to hear other things about the celebrity, so ask on their behalf. For example, if a famous singer is promoting a new book of poems they have written, ask if they will be going back into the studio to record another album.

Everyday interviews

It does not matter whom you are interviewing, brief yourself thoroughly on who they are, where they are from and what they represent. Likewise, they must know who you are, and who you represent, so always identify yourself and the station you work for before arranging an interview.

'You're going to have to speak up, young lady.'

Sound levels

When doing a sound-level check, ask the interviewee to say and spell their name (and title or job description if they have one). This is a casual, friendly way of making sure you have their details right.

Short and simple

Consider your questions well in advance of the interview and what you want to achieve from it. You do not need to write them down and read them off a paper – that looks very amateurish to the interviewee. It is a good idea to keep them short, simple and to the point; but be flexible; the answers you get could open up a whole new line of enquiry and set the interview off on a tangent. You can steer the interview back to the main points later. In the same vein, you may ask a question that the interviewee has already covered. This shows both the interviewee and the listener that you are not listening.

There are instances where you should be firm and stay true to the questions you have set. Politicians, for example, are notorious for saying as much as they can and will control the course of the interview if you let them. Be on your guard against this, and politely but firmly continue your line of questioning. Stay in control, be professional, do not be overawed and, above all, *listen*.

Don't rehearse

If the interviewee stipulates a need to know just what sort of ground you hope to cover in the interview, by all means tell them. Do not, however, tell them the questions you will be asking, or rehearse the interview with them.

Warm-up

A really good reporter can put an interviewee at ease by what is known as a warm-up. You may not have long to perform a warm-up in some situations, but in time you will find it will come naturally.

You have to show that you are calm and in control. The interviewee may well be a little nervous, especially if they are not used to speaking to a reporter. If you greet someone with a smile (providing it is a happy situation) and make eye contact with them and you are open with your body language and gestures, you will relax the interviewee. If you have your arms folded or hands stuffed in your pockets and look at them through sunglasses, they're hardly going to relax or be open with you.

Microphones and recorders can unnerve an interviewee. Put your subject at ease by explaining something about the equipment you will be using, how long you expect the interview to take and so on. In an effort to please, do not be tempted to play the interview back for them. Some people do not like hearing their voices played back over a recorder so that far from being happy, they may ask for the recording to be redone or insist on editing bits out.

If you are a lot taller than the interviewee, lessen your height by suggesting that you do the interview sitting down. Be courteous and considerate at all times: do not intimidate the interviewee by towering over them or patronize them by bending down as if you were speaking to a child.

Warm-down

The 'warm-down' at the end of the interview is aptly titled because that is just what it should be. Smile and thank the interviewee for their effort and time taken in talking to you. Leave them feeling valued and appreciated. You cannot just say, 'Thanks. Bye!' and turn your back and run for the studio. Continue to talk to your interviewee with casual conversation as you pack your equipment up, just as you would a friend. You may be in a hurry with deadlines to meet and this may be your umpteenth interview of the day, but do not be tempted to dash away. When planning interviews, always include a bit of time for this warm-down period. Handled with care, you will make friends and contacts who will continue to listen to your station and follow your career with interest.

Tricky questions

Do consider your listeners when formulating questions. If you are questioning the agriculture minister, ask the question the farmer wants an answer to, not what the minister might want to be asked. If you have time to plan ahead, call a farmer you know and ask if there is anything they might suggest.

Avoid presenting yourself as some sort of crusader battling for the rights of your listeners. The job of the reporter is to put questions and get answers on behalf of listeners, not take on the mantle of grand inquisitor.

Some questions beg obvious answers: 'How does it feel?' put to the lottery winner or to the soccer captain who has just lost the match, deserve the contempt they get. At best, the answer will be monosyllabic; at worst the listeners will throw their radios out of the window in disgust. Be imaginative when asking questions by trying to place yourself in the interviewee's position. As a lottery winner or match loser, what questions would you want to be asked?

Keep your questions simple but pertinent to the situation. Overlong and complex questions sound clever, but they can confuse the interviewee and the listeners.

Providing you stay clear of leading questions, such as: 'Do you catch this bus every day?', you won't get monosyllabic yes or no answers. It is better to ask: 'How do you think the bus service can be improved?'

Some interviewees may try to mask their answers in jargon if they do not want you or the listeners to understand. Or maybe, they are so used to speaking in jargon, they don't know they are doing it. If you do not understand the answer, don't be afraid to ask the interviewee to explain what they mean.

As a final point, ask the interviewee if there is anything they would like to add. If there is not, be sure in your own mind that you have covered all the points you wanted to. You may not have a chance to ask again.

Remember, it is not the interviewee's responsibility to provide you with an interesting interview – that responsibility lies firmly with you.

In conclusion, in order to conduct an interview:
- Brief yourself
- Control the interview
- Be brief
- Be alert
- Expand and explain
- Is there anything else?

Editing

Whether you are editing material on a computer's audio software program or splicing quarter-inch tape, the principles of editing are the same. Experienced journalists will tell you that editing actually begins in the mind long before you reach the newsroom. During the interview you will begin to hear things you know can be cut and therefore make a mental note of them. The more you do it, the easier this process becomes.

The first edit you make should be on the disc or tape. With mini-discs you can make your first edit on the disc by 'cutting and pasting', putting track markers in and deleting unwanted material using the in-built edit facility. You can even take out ums and ers. On tape recorders, you can dub-edit. Connect your machine to another tape recorder and dub off only the material you want to use in the order you want to use it.

During the editing process, it is most important to make positive editorial decisions. Assemble the bits you want according to

Figure 15.4

chronological order, making sure to time the whole piece. Once you have done this 'rough edit' you can start the process of 'fine editing,' which means cutting out the coughs, ums and ers, and irrelevant phrases. On a PC, you can do this using an audio software program; if you are editing on a tape recorder, you will be working with quarter-inch reel tape.

Remember the 'atmosphere' you recorded when you did your interview? You may want to use that now in order to give the piece a natural sound quality by dubbing it onto a second track, or as part of the intro or outro. It can help to set the scene.

Don't be too hasty to cut out all the ums and ers. It is important that you retain the meaning of what is being said. If you take out a long pause, or remove some faltering remarks, you alter the entire meaning and the context within which it was originally spoken. To do so is highly unethical and unjust to your interviewee and listeners. As an example of this, consider the following interview with an Anglican bishop:

Int: *Do you think the ordination of women into the Anglican Church has been successful?*

Bishop: (Long pause followed by an intake of breath) *Yes.*

The long pause and intake of breath suggests the bishop has obviously thought long and hard about the subject and this shows in his reply. If you were to cut the pause and intake of breath so that he instantly replies yes, it appears as if the bishop has never given it a second thought. Consequently, you have altered the 'personality' of the speaker – which will offend him and surprise those closest to him. When a journalist is unscrupulous and wilfully assembles an edit with the aim of altering the original contents, or because they are too lazy to do otherwise, they do a lot of damage to the reputation of the interviewee and the views they hold. It also reflects badly on journalism – which people should be able to trust. In short, it is a misrepresentation that benefits no one and is simply reprehensible.

In the past, journalists editing on tape machines made sure they threw nothing away before completing the package. Make sure you don't throw anything away and check each edit before moving on to the next, just in case you have made a mistake.

The vox pop

Abbreviated from the Latin *vox populi*, the voice of the people, when you have mastered editing a conventional interview, the vox pop will really test your skills and patience.

In broadcasting terms, vox pops are a montage of various people's voices, each expressing in just a few words their reaction to an item in the news. The vox pop must be relevant; it should not be done simply to fill air time. The subject might be serious or tongue-in-cheek; you might talk to three people or 33. The object of the vox pop works well in local radio, because it reflects how some people feel over an issue that directly affects their local community. Listeners can relate (or not) to the feelings of their neighbours.

The principle is to pose one question to various people in the street or at a place of work. You might ask: 'Do you think women make better drivers?' (a question that relates to news that women drivers are statistically safer than men). If the interviewee is responsive, by all means ask supplementary questions such as: 'Why do you think so?' or 'How can men improve their driving?' Do not ask a multitude of questions, or the vox pop will take twice as long to complete and be difficult to edit. Some people will answer the question with a wry smile; others may take it deadly seriously.

Whatever the response, be sure to get a rich mixture of voices and reactions.

Take care with the microphone. There is not time to adjust recording levels each time if you are using a tape recorder, so make sure you hold the microphone close enough to pick up varying levels of voice.

It is a good idea to try to ensure that local accents are represented in a vox pop. In some large towns and cities, it may be that everyone you approach speaks with a Standard English accent or other regional accents. Local people can feel left out if they do not hear their accent represented so where possible include a few examples.

As with conventional interview techniques, be open and honest when stopping people to talk. Tell them what you are doing and the radio station you are from, and if people do not want to talk, do not try to make them.

If the response is not as polite as you would want, or it does not agree with your own views, try not to grimace or argue. Keep smiling, turn to the next person and get on with the job in hand. You will find people's reactions will vary depending on the day of the week (few people like Mondays), the weather, the season and the time of day. If people look as if they do not want to be approached, leave them. Even if you intend to use only three or four voices, talk to 23 at least to get a good cross-section of people of all ages and from all walks of life. From these, you can pick the best. Most vox pops occupy only about a minute of airtime, so be as selective as possible.

When choosing a place to record your vox pop, be careful there is not too much noise from traffic or other background noise, as it can detract from what people are saying and make the piece difficult to edit.

During the assembly of your edit, listen out for contrasting voices, which you can place one after the other. Pay particular attention to any comments that might be considered slanderous or in bad taste. The odd mild swear word might be acceptable, but always seek advice if you want to leave it in.

Finally, depending on the nature of the vox pop, place an appropriate comment at the end of the piece that sums up people's feelings; it might be something humorous or thought-provoking. For a serious piece, this can be difficult. You need to find a comment that encapsulates the feelings of those affected, not something that flippantly tries to make light of the situation. And when writing your cue, do not make out that the vox pop represents the majority voice of the community, it does not.

Writing cues

A cue (or link) acts as an introduction to a report or interview, and is read by the newsreader or presenter. Generally, the length of the cue for news reports should not exceed one minute, or for a programme feature, three minutes. However, this does vary depending on station policy.

Provided the story is comprehensible to the listener – in other words contains plenty of relevant facts – the shorter the cue is, the better. However, it should not be too short. In order for the listener to adjust their attention to a new story, the cue needs to carry several lines of fact. One-line cues do not work: 'The chancellor is to put another penny on income tax. John Doh reports.' You need to alert the listener before you can inform them.

The purpose of the cue is to:

- alert the listener to a new item
- introduce the report or item
- give extra information or updates, perhaps from other sources or stories.

The cue should provide sufficient information on the background of the story for the listener to understand even if the report fails due to technical or human error.

In addition to acting as an audible warning to the listener, the cue also sets out operating instructions for the newsreader, producer or engineer. When writing a cue, include the following:

- A catchline (title) of one word to identify the story which should be the same as that used by the accompanying audio report.

- The date and time of writing (identifies the freshness of the report for later bulletins).
- Your name or initials as author. If it is an agency source, include their name.
- At the foot of the cue write: CUT (this signifies the end of the spoken cue and the beginning of the audio report or interview) followed by title (or number), duration of the cut and the out cue (the last few words of the audio report).

Example

BOXER   7 Apr/14:30   jd/townchester newsagency

World heavyweight boxing champion Butch Basher is visiting Townchester today to open a new fitness centre. Basher, who won the world championship title earlier this year when he knocked out Nosher Nuckle in five rounds, is in the middle of a nationwide promotional tour. The boxer is no stranger to Townchester, having spent his early career as a jobbing builder for a local firm. Our reporter, John Doh, met up with him at the fitness centre:

CUT/Boxer

Dur: 30"

Out: 'hope to return soon'

The three-minute feature

Features are a mix of educational and entertaining items that can be used in a magazine programme. Like the print magazine feature, radio features look at the story behind the story.

The term 'three-minute feature' remains from the 1930s when features were first introduced. The early recording machines used a disc that could only accommodate items of three minutes or less. Although no such limitations exist today, people have grown accustomed to the short, informative feature. Some stations may use longer or shorter features depending on their policy, but generally three minutes is long enough. Not every subject is going to be of universal interest, and the shorter it is, the more time there is available for other subjects.

Producing a feature is a great challenge for a journalist and it can make a change from the everyday news reports. You can always instigate a feature idea taken from a news report you have covered. There may be something about the subject of a particular news item that would make a great feature if it were expanded upon.

Because of the time constraint, it is not possible to tackle immensely complex issues. Therefore the subject should be straightforward and you need a clear idea about what it is you want to say. Before suggesting it to the editor or producer, write your idea down on paper in as few words as possible. For example:

> *Townchester Corporation engineer Pete McGeet is to test a pioneering device that will save thousands of people from being killed or injured by land-mines. The feature will explain how he invented it, how he will test it and to whom he hopes to sell it.*

This feature example has three parts, so you would need to allow a maximum of one minute for each part: the first explaining how Pete invented the device; the second about the testing; and the third about the people he hopes to sell it to. You need to talk to more than one person to get a contrasting voice, so perhaps a representative from one of the land-mine clearance organizations could offer an opinion as could a representative from a company with an interest in buying it.

Because of its subject matter, the feature could be overloaded with information, but some tight editing should do it. It is easy to record too much information and then have difficulty editing to the required three minutes. Always think about how to close a feature and how it might be cued; the cue is particularly important because it 'sells' the idea to the listener.

Actuality is very important in radio. In your feature on land-mines, you will need to record a lot of your sound in the environment where McGeet works when creating his device. If he uses drills or a specific tool, record the sound of him using it. To demonstrate the impact of land-mines, you could use the sound of an explosion or two. It may not be possible to record an actual mine exploding, but the chances are there will be a sound effects recording held in the station's library. If there is, make sure it is a land-mine explosion and not the sound of a shell impacting. If you cut corners and use anything else, you might be surprised at how many listeners will call the station correcting you for not using the right sound.

Music can also be used if it is appropriate and relevant. However, do not use it to make light of a serious issue. Features are, and should be, educational and entertaining in what they deliver to the radio audience. It is the entertainment value within a feature that makes it work so well by catching the ear of the listener. Just remember that the message is always of greater importance than the medium.

The package

Interviews and features are a great way of conveying material provided the subject is interesting and the interviewee is articulate. Where this is not the case, or you have more than one interviewee, the 'package' (or wrap) can be the answer.

Creating the package is very much like putting together a mini-programme with its studio links and prerecorded inserts. With some deft editing, you can put together a very entertaining package – but do make sure that it conveys the point you are trying to put across. The best way of doing this is to convey the message as simply as possible.

Writing news bulletins

The techniques for writing news bulletins are quite different from those you would use for writing a newspaper report. Firstly, you are writing words to be heard, so they need to be clear and concise. You are also writing words that can be read and spoken easily by the newsreader – which may be you. Whereas words in a newspaper article can be reread if at first they do not make sense, with a radio bulletin there is never a second opportunity for the listener. A complex, wordy statement is likely to confuse and cause the listener to tune out or turn off.

There are, of course, some components that are necessary to all news writing, whatever the medium. The leading sentence must be attention-grabbing and informative:

> *Townchester stone quarry is to close with the loss of over two hundred and fifty jobs ...*

This leading sentence attracts the attention of the listener and explains what is happening. Even if radio reception was lost to the listener immediately afterwards, the message has got through, which is more than the following sentence would achieve:

> *Townchester stone quarry, which is owned by the Acme Stone Corporation, announced earlier today ...*

Radio does not necessarily have a listener's full attention. It may be on as an accompaniment whilst the listener does other things, so the importance of grabbing their attention is paramount. And once their attention has been gained, the story needs to be repeated and told in full.

Radio news usually begins with the newsreader announcing the headlines. These will be one-line sentences that forewarn the listener of items to follow in the bulletin. An intro might read something like this:

> *Radio Local news at ten o'clock, I'm John Doh.*

> *Townchester stone quarry is to close with the loss of over two hundred and fifty jobs.*

> *The county's farmers protest outside local supermarkets.*

> *And Townchester Hall's famous statue is to get a face-lift.*

After a brief pause or news jingle, the bulletin is read in full.

> *The closure of Townchester stone quarry with the loss of over two-hundred and fifty jobs has been announced by its owners, Acme Stone Corporation, after many weeks of speculation. The quarry, which has been producing the world famous Townchester stone for three hundred years, is said to have reached its production limit, according to a*

*corporation spokesperson. Proposals to extend the quarry
were turned down two years ago after protests from
environmental groups and residents whose property values
would have been affected by further development. Acme
Stone Corporation hope to place most of the workforce in
vacancies at other quarries in the area.*

In the 'quarry' story, the listener is told immediately of the loss of
250 jobs which has been expected – hence the 'speculation'. This
is followed by an explanation from an un-named spokesperson
representing the owners and a brief history of its place as a stone
supplier. The story ends on a more optimistic note with the hope
that workers will be found jobs at other quarries.

The story is brief and to the point and sums up the main points as
they are known at the time. Of course, within the hour, there may
be developments to update the story. Even if someone tunes in part
way through the transmission of the story, the second part makes
mention of the Acme Stone Corporation and their hope in placing
jobs elsewhere, so it is still possible to make sense of the story's
main point – quarry closure.

Facts and figures in a story should be clarified and made simple to
understand. If you find it difficult to read or understand, you can be
sure that the listener will find it difficult to understand too.

In most cases, when reading figures, it is better to say 'nearly ten
per cent' or 'almost one in ten' rather than 9.8 per cent. A sum of
money such as £4,895 can be spoken as being 'nearly five-thousand
pounds'. Where it is possible to do so, repeat and explain figures in
full to avoid confusion. For example:

*... spending will go up by nearly fifteen per cent adding ten
million pounds to government expenditure. The estimated
cost to the tax payer will be an extra twenty pounds a year.*

It is the 'twenty pounds a year' that listeners will be particularly
interested in. Also, write figures as words; this prevents a mistake
when reading figures, especially long figures in the hundreds of
thousands or millions. You may be writing the bulletin, but
someone else could be reading it.

Whereas a writer for a quality newspaper can use quite complex sentence structure as part of the paper's preferred style, the radio newswriter cannot:

A survey in the industry's magazine, Vision, shows an overwhelming view that programmes are becoming more and more offensive.

This sentence works well in newsprint but not so well over the radio. For a start, try saying 'in the industry'. Not only is it not so easy to say, but the listener might think you are saying something else: 'indy industry', perhaps. It is one thing to be able to see a word, but simply to hear it briefly can result in mistaking its meaning or context. Some words are too similar to others in sound; others are too complex.

For radio, it is a good idea to avoid certain words. The following is a list of suggestions, clichés and journalese – words that should be avoided when writing a bulletin:

- ■ **Age** – A person's age is not normally relevant in a news bulletin unless it refers to special circumstances: 'An eight-year-old girl is recovering in hospital after an emergency operation ...'
- ■ **Attacked** – Use in the context of reporting a physical attack. Use 'criticized' if it refers to a verbal confrontation.
- ■ **Axed** – Use 'made redundant' or 'cut'.
- ■ **Banned** – sounds like 'band'. Use 'outlawed' or 'prohibited'.
- ■ **Battle** – Preferably, use 'argue' or 'dispute' for verbal confrontation, or 'fight to keep' depending on context.
- ■ **Best/biggest** – In whose opinion? Always precede with 'claimed to be'.
- ■ **Bid** – Better to use 'attempt(ed)' rather than 'prison escape bid'. 'Bid' for auctions or gambling
- ■ **Billion** – Sounds too much like 'million'. Better to state the equivalent in millions.
- ■ **Boost** – Tabloid journalese. Use 'increase'.

- **Boss** – Sounds dictatorial and old-fashioned. Replace with: 'managing director'; 'manager'; 'employer'; 'chairperson' or 'chair'.

- **Catastrophe/catastrophic** – You may think something is catastrophic; your listeners may not. Loss of life can be catastrophic; the failure of a racing yacht to perform, is not.

- **Centre** – Be sure the argument centres *on*, not around.

- **Chiefs** – In Britain, the terms are chief fire officer, chief of police, etc. Not fire chief or police chief. Health 'chiefs' are administrators or officials.

- **Clash** – Belongs in the tabloids. Use 'argument'; 'debate'; 'dispute'; 'altercation'; 'difference of opinion'.

- **Crisis** – Implies a value judgement. Use it only in the context of a quote.

- **Crunch** – Clichéd. Also sounds like a breakfast cereal.

- **Dead on arrival** – Tabloid journalese also used in Hollywood movies. If it is known the victim died on the way to hospital, then say so. Always avoid euphemisms. If someone has died or been killed, say so.

- **Death toll** – Better to say: 'brings the total killed to five hundred', or whatever.

- **Draconian** – Use sparingly and in its proper sense. 'Harsh' or 'severe' are normally more accurate.

- **Due to** – 'The road is closed due to gas repairs'. Replace with 'because of'. ('Due to' also means 'scheduled to'.)

- **Eleventh hour/last ditch** – Both hackneyed, so try 'final attempt' or 'one last try'

- **Enormity** – Although technically it can be used to describe enormous size, avoid it.

- **Fighting for life** – Is very emotive and may be inaccurate by definition. Use 'critically ill'.

- **Full-scale** – Better to say exactly what this all-encompassing term means. If the police are using 500 officers to search woodland, then say so.
- **Gutted** – Use only as part of a quote: 'The team's manager told our reporter he was "gutted" by the result.' Otherwise, use 'disappointed'.
- **Helping police with their inquiries** – This is police jargon and may look all right in print but for radio it is better to say: 'being questioned by police' or 'being interviewed by police'.
- **Handicapped** – Use in respect of horseracing or professional golf tournaments but never in relation to a person's physical or mental condition.
- **Huge** – Just how huge is huge? This non-specific word should be used sparingly.
- **Hyperbole** – A relative newcomer to media vocabulary, meaning an exaggerated statement that is not to be taken literally. There are two problems with this word: it is rarely used in ordinary conversation, and a vox pop might show that many people are not familiar with its meaning. Also, when seen on paper, the temptation is to pronounce it 'hyperbowl'.
- **Imply/infer** – Don't confuse the two: a speaker implies something; the hearer infers what is said.
- **Inflation** – Is a rate, not an absolute, so it needs a time-scale: 'the annual rate of inflation', for example.
- **Irony** – Don't confuse with 'contrast', 'paradox' or 'coincidence'. Irony is a rather subtle concept, so avoid its use.
- **Jokes** – If the news is quirky, then let it speak for itself. Never try to write comedy into a news script.
- **Less** – 'Less of a burden'; 'less trouble'; 'less sugar'. The word refers to quantity only. When referring to numbers, use 'fewer', as in 'fewer police on the streets'. People are always referred to as numbers, not quantities.

- **Literally** – Means just what it says; it cannot be used as a metaphor. If you refer to a marathon runner thus: 'He literally flew down the final half-mile', you are saying that he actually did fly the final half-mile in what the listener could only assume to be an aeroplane.
- **Major** – As in 'important'; can be overused and often overstated. Be careful.
- **Massive** – Just like 'huge', the word is non-specific, and it is better to be specific.
- **Meanwhile** – Meanwhile should only be used to describe concurrent events: 'Mr Blair met his new Foreign Secretary at Number Ten. Meanwhile, his new Chancellor was talking to reporters next door.'
- **Meantime** – A novice announcer once read on air: 'The time is twenty-two hundred hours, green witch. [confused pause] Mean time, here is the news …' What they should have said was: 'The time is twenty-two hundred hours, Greenwich Mean Time. Here is the news …' The moral of this true story is, read what you write and write what you read.
- **Mercy dash/ mercy mission** – Great for tabloids, not for radio.
- **Miracle** – Use only within a quote: 'Friends said his recovery was nothing less than a miracle'. Otherwise, the correct adjective is 'miraculous'.
- **Non-payment of** – Is legal jargon and is better replaced with 'not paying'.
- **Oust** – Works better in tabloids and is too close in sound to 'out' for use on radio.
- **Plea** – Use in court reports to describe a legal process. Otherwise, use sparingly.
- **Probe** – Doctors and engineers use probes; the police, politicians and radio journalists do not.
- **Press conference** – Is an old-fashioned term. Use 'news conference' because journalists from all branches of the media attend.

- **Quiz** – Police do not 'quiz'; they interview, question or interrogate.
- **Refute** – This word looks better in print. When spoken in a bulletin it might confuse as it sounds like 'dispute' or 'refuse'. Often wrongly used: it means to prove that something is wrong; it does not mean 'disagree' or 'deny'.
- **Row** – Frequently overused, so try an alternative such as 'argument'; 'debate'; 'discussion'; 'dispute' or 'difference of opinion'. There is also a danger that the newsreader will pronounce it wrongly, as 'roe'.
- **Rushed** – This is another overused term: 'The victim was rushed by ambulance to the nearest hospital'. Try 'taken to'.
- **Sensational** – A word loved by tabloid editors and disc jockeys. And because they love it, you should avoid it when presenting serious news – unless you want to use 'popfantastic' as well.
- **Set** – Dinner tables are set; jellies set; game, set and match. 'Councillor Doh is set to step into a row', is pure journalese and should be left to the tabloids.
- **Shot in the arm** – Clichés like this one can so easily be mistaken for a literal meaning: a bullet wound or even a drug addict's needle. Avoid.
- **Shock** – A great word for the tabloid page as it stands out in print. For radio, 'surprise' or 'unexpected' are better.
- **Sniffer-dogs/tracker-dog**s – Where dogs are used by police and customs officials, use the term 'dogs' or 'specially trained dogs'.
- **So-called** – Sounds sceptical and patronizing. 'Widely known as' or 'usually known as' are better descriptive terms.
- **Spark off/trigger** – Clichés to be avoided.
- **Swoop** – Hawks swoop. Unless police fly in to arrest someone, they most certainly never 'swoop'. It is better to use an alternative such as 'raid'.

- **Top-level** – Do not use any more than you have to.
- **Total(ly)** – Tautological, as in 'total write-off'; 'totally gutted' or 'totally extinguished'. Leave it totally and utterly alone.
- **Tragedy** – Means a person's downfall through his or her own actions. Modern usage has widened the definition, but it might be better to avoid when referring to accidents and disasters.
- **Try** – Try to remember this: you try *to* do something; you do not try *and* do it.
- **Vital** – Is it really vital? Or is it just 'important'.
- **Vow** – Something you do in a court of law, or at the altar. In any other context, use 'promise', 'threat' or simply 'say'.
- **Walkabout** – This Australian word translated from the Aboriginal referred originally to going walkabout in the outback. The term is overused by the media and should be considered long and hard before using.
- **Whirlwind tour** – Used for short-term royal and political tours, this cliché is not easy to replace, but worth a try.
- **Widespread anxiety** – Says who? Always define news content and avoid generalities.

Jargon

Many news releases coming into the station's newsroom will contain jargon from press officers representing trades and professions. They sometimes forget that not everyone will be familiar with specific professional terms. Ironically, a certain amount of jargon has been adopted by journalists for use as buzzwords to pep up a dull report, and consequently they seep through into everyday use and become clichéd.

The following sentence is quite often heard on news broadcasts: 'A man is helping police with their inquiries'. This is despite the possibility that he is not being at all helpful. In such cases, jargon is vague, so replace it with more descriptive alternatives wherever you can.

Reported speech

When you quote a person, start the sentence with their name and designation. This gives an idea of how much importance you should give their statement, and rolls more fluently from the tongue.

Mr Blair says there'll be no more tax cuts in the next budget.

Alternatively:

The Prime Minister says …

Butchers say the price of lamb is going up next week.

Never:

There'll be no tax cuts in the next budget. That's according to the Prime Minster.

Never:

The price of lamb is going up next week, say butchers.

Tenses

Radio is now, so present news in the present tense.

The mayor of Townchester says she'll oppose cuts in public spending.

Not:

The mayor of Townchester said last night she'd oppose cuts in public spending.

Use 'today' sparingly; the listener will assume that what you are telling them happened today, unless you say otherwise.

Contractions

Speech should always be natural and reflect common usage, so do not be afraid to use normal contractions: it'll, that'll, there'll, who'd, couldn't, would've, and so on.

The only exception to this is where special emphasis is needed. For example:

Farmer Jones says the subsidy will not be enough.

Abbreviations

Well-known abbreviations such as RAF, TUC, BBC and RSPCA, need no explanation. Less-known abbreviations such as the NUM (National Union of Mineworkers) will require explanation. You do not need to give the abbreviation in full, just clarify:

> *The government are holding talks with the miners' union –*
> *the NUM.*

Reading news bulletins on air

One of the most exciting parts of radio journalism is getting the chance to read a news bulletin live on air. Many listeners hold the misconception that radio newsreaders are a bit like cuckoos in a clock: all they need do is deliver a news announcement every hour and then curl up with a book and cup of coffee until it is time to announce again. If only it were so.

Local news bulletins are read by journalists as part of their weekly duty roster. In the morning, you might be interviewing several people and following up other stories; but by the afternoon it could be your turn to read the bulletins. It is not necessary to have a 'golden' voice or a BBC-type Standard English accent; provided you do not rush your speech and that you enunciate properly, you will make a fine newsreader. There are some techniques to be acquired, and these cannot be learnt overnight.

Putting news in order

Not as easy as it sounds. What seems important to you may not be important to someone else. Priorities will vary from bulletin to bulletin. The lead story at 9 am may not be the lead story 60 minutes later because of changed priorities. Remember that it is people who make news, so items featuring death, redundancy, rescues, awards, all come high on the agenda.

National news precedes local news. To begin with, always seek advice when putting a bulletin together regardless of how comprehensive your training has been.

Driving the desk

Training courses teach student journalists how to 'drive' a desk. Do bear in mind, however, that when you start your new job at the station, the desk might be very different from the one you used at college. Ask if you can familiarize yourself with the desk at the earliest opportunity. You may need to familiarize yourself with a PC, 'carts' (audio-cartridges) and cart machines, telephones, CD players, turntables, tape decks, reel-to-reel machines and faders that open and close the other way from the ones you have been used to.

Even if you have been used to fiddling with and resetting knobs and buttons at college, don't *ever* touch them (without authorization) when you start work. They will have been carefully set up by an engineer who will not be pleased if you alter the delicate balance of the desk or other machines. Provided your mouth is no more or less than a hand-span from the microphone, you should not need to adjust levels.

Do not bring hot or cold beverages (with the exception of a glass of water placed out of harm's way) or food of any description into the studio, and especially to place on the desk. Nor should you lounge back and place your feet on the desk. In many stations, these are misdemeanours of the highest order that can result in your being dismissed.

Sitting comfortably

Place the loose headline sheets on the desk in front of you and in order, so that when you open the microphone all you need do is lift each sheet as necessary. Drop each sheet to the floor once you have read from it; this is to prevent a sheet from obscuring a fader or gauge, or confusing you if you look away to attend to something else, then turn back and pick up a sheet you have already used. Curl up the bottom-right corner of each page so that it is easy to separate from the rest. Make sure you have the entire bulletin.

Exercise your voice before speaking. Read the bulletin through once or twice – even if you did write it – as this checks for errors and loosens the voice. Also try a tongue-twister or two to exercise the tongue (see the suggestions in the section 'Preparing to speak' in Chapter 14).

Keep a pen and pencil handy as you may get a phone call to update an item just before you go on air.

Sit upright. This posture helps the diaphragm to work more easily, enabling you to deliver the lines more effectively. Relax your mind and muscles; take a good breath so that you are not running short of breath between lines. Blow your nose and clear your throat – you do not want any congested airways half-way through a bulletin. Be ready to play the news jingle and open the microphone as soon as you get the audible cue to broadcast from the presenter whose show is currently being broadcast. They may be in the next studio or 50 miles away. The chances are, you will be in a studio alone.

Attacking a bulletin

Experienced newsreaders make reading bulletins seem fiendishly easy. It isn't. You need to modulate your voice so that you speak at a constant level, but without droning. You must not give a bulletin dramatic impact either; it is not your job to act.

When writing the bulletin, emphasize key words by writing them in upper case. You will then know to 'attack' these words when you speak. Also, make sure there is plenty of space between paragraphs and a partial dividing line to separate items. You can roughly time the bulletin by calculating that it takes one second to speak three words.

Example

The TUC is calling for a minimum wage of FIVE POUNDS FORTY an hour.

Its annual conference in Glasgow has been told it's the only answer to ruthless employers, who are returning workers to the exploitation of the Dickensian era.

—o—

Mortgage payments are being cut following today's half per cent drop in interest rates.

Two big building societies ... the Finsbury and the Colchester Midland ... are reducing home-loan rates by POINT-FOUR per cent. The move's been triggered by a signal from the Bank of England, bringing down interest rates to ten-and-a-half per cent.

---○---

MUGLEYDONIAN troops and SETSIBAN guerrillas have cut
Mugleydonia in TWO ... in a battle which has isolated much of
the breakaway republic.

PLATSIBAN security-forces are reportedly RETREATING towards
the capital – ZANZIDU – after suffering heavy losses in fierce
fighting.

Listen to an experienced newsreader at your station or on a national
radio station. Pay special attention to their delivery and timing –
which is so important if the bulletin is to be read within the allotted
timeframe of two or three minutes. Each item requires a slight
pause to separate it from the last, and each has to be attacked with
fresh emphasis, otherwise the listener will not know where the last
item ended and the next begins. Importantly, it must flow.

In order to make it flow, practise your delivery (off air) whenever
you get an opportunity. The more you practise, the better your
delivery will become. Much also depends on how well the bulletin
is written. Avoid lengthy sentences and use a straightforward term
as opposed to a complex one.

Foreign words and names can be daunting if you are not sure how
to pronounce them. Always seek advice first and foremost.
Whatever you do, don't try to be clever by pronouncing a word as
if you were a native of that country. Doing so can slow the tempo
of your delivery, not to mention sound odd or partisan if you cannot
treat every foreign word or name similarly. At best, it sounds comic
and detracts from the message. Leave acting to actors.

Finally, leave the studio as you would wish to find it: clear up your
papers and remove any carts you have used. Be sure to shut the
door behind you.

Freelance opportunities

Generally, freelance radio journalists come from a background of
staff positions in radio journalism and have built up a lot of
contacts and experience.

If you intend to follow a freelance career, it is important to contact radio producers and station managers first to see if there is any possibility they might use your material, and if so, what subject material they might need. If they give you a chance to prove yourself, they may not want to pay you much – probably just enough to reimburse you for the discs or tapes you have bought. Even then, there may be no promise to use anything you send them. The best way to break in may be to record news items that the station journalists cannot get to, rather than putting time and money into producing three-minute features. Some stations use freelances for court reporting; however, you must hold a National Certificate to report from law courts. Apart from courts, journalists have most events covered, so the chances of scooping the staffers and other freelances are rare.

Should you feel it worth doing, it will be necessary to buy your own quality recording equipment. Brand new mini-disc recorders can be bought from high street retailers for about £150. Broadcast-quality microphones can be much more expensive depending on whether you buy new or secondhand.

You should not part with too much money for a secondhand tape machine, as the mini-disc has made these items largely obsolete. You will not normally find them on flea markets but may see them advertised in specialist hi-fi magazines. Bear in mind that as mini-discs are reasonably priced, and their quality superb, older tape machines may not be worth the price being asked.

To edit your tapes, it is worth investing in a software audio package for your PC. However, these are not cheap. If you buy an old-fashioned reel-to-reel tape recorder, make sure it has the facility to record two tracks and the capacity to run at a speed of 15 IPS (inches per second). This gives you as editor much more leeway in cutting out a sigh or breath in someone's speech.

With some good, original ideas and perseverance, it is not impossible to become a freelance radio journalist. It helps if you have some good quality, reliable equipment, of course. The best time to start establishing a reputation is when you are a media student – when you have access to good equipment and can demonstrate to local stations that you are starting out and serious in your attempt. Also, try entering competitions that are sometimes announced by the BBC. Both national and local radio stations will post details of forthcoming competitions to local press and colleges in addition to broadcasting details. The regional art councils may also know of opportunities for interesting 'sound works'.

For the contact book

Broadcast Journalism Training Council (BJTC)
39 Westbourne Gardens
London W2 5NR
Tel: 020 7727 9522
Fax: 020 7727 9522
E-mail: secretary@bjtc.org.uk
Internet: www.bjtc.org.uk

Community Media Association
Head Office
15 Paternoster Row
Sheffield S1 2BX
Tel: 0114 279 5219
Fax: 0114 279 8976
E-mail: cma@commedia.org.uk

London office:
356 Holloway Road
London N7 6PA
Tel: 020 7700 0100 ex 234
Fax: 020 7700 0099
E-mail: cmalondon@commedia.org.uk
Internet: www.commedia.org.uk

The Radio Academy
5 Market Place
London W1N 7AH
Tel: 020 7255 2010
Fax: 020 7255 2029
E-mail: info@radioacademy.org
Internet: www.radioacademy.org

Books

Andrew Boyd, *Broadcast Journalism – Techniques of Radio and TV News* (4th edition). Focal Press, 1997
Contents include: newsgathering; interviewing; radio news coverage; and much more.

Paul Chantler and Sim Harris, *Local Radio Journalism* (2nd edition). Focal Press, 1997
Contents include: the news bulletin; the structure of local radio; the radio reporter; newsdesk management; specialist programmes; and much more.

Lawrie Douglas, Marie Kinsey and Linda Gage (eds), *Guide to Commercial Radio Journalism* (2nd edition). Focal Press, 1998
Contents include: using the equipment; writing for radio; programme production; restrictions on reporting; and much more.

Peter Wilby and Andy Conroy, *The Radio Handbook*. Routledge, 1994

16 | INTERVIEW WITH CAROLINE HODGSON

Caroline, 24, is a radio journalist and has been working for a local independent radio station in West Sussex since 1998. She has a BA honours degree in journalism studies and a postgraduate diploma in Broadcast Journalism – both qualifications attained from her studies at Falmouth College of Art, Cornwall.

Q   *How did you learn of the job vacancy with your current station?*

CH   I learnt of the vacancy while I was doing some placement work with a radio station in Bristol. The wonders of IRN – Independent Radio News – they have a system where you can send scripts and requests, and one of them was for a journalist at an independent station in West Sussex. Then it's a case of going through the usual channels, sending a demo tape, CV and then attending an interview.

Q   *What is your job title at the station?*

CH   I haven't got one as such. For official purposes, it's 'broadcast journalist', but I'm a news editor in the afternoons – my shift starts at 11 am and finishes about 7 pm. And at weekends, I'm the only person so it's a case of doing everything. There are just two people here on a Sunday – me and the presenter.

Q   *Were you well prepared for your first day in the job?*

CH   I was really nervous because all of a sudden it was the big wide world. As clichéd as it sounds, it's different when you really have to work against the clock, rather than just doing it in practice. I had a week's induction, which was a brilliant idea and helped me enormously. So I'd already had a week's 'training'. But even my first day doing that, I was incredibly scared because there was so much to understand and get to grips with.

Q   *Did your course work prepare you for this?*

CH   As far as my course work had gone, I felt as prepared as I could have been – obviously I had no experience – so, I think that's where I was lacking the most.

Q   *Tell me about your daily tasks.*

CH   It varies. People can say to me, 'What are you doing at twelve minutes past two?' and I'll be able to tell them what I'll be doing on the dot. My tasks change daily because of the content, but everything is the same. I could do it with my eyes closed now. I come in and help with the lunchtime news programme. I don't often present that, sometimes I do. I do interviews and edit and write up the cues, or I'll be doing something simple like the 'check' calls to make sure we're not missing anything in the area from the police, fire or ambulance services. I take over at half past one when the news editor goes home. I'm in complete charge and use my discretion as to what goes in the afternoon news. I spend the time rewriting scripts, doing interviews for that day or the next, and editing. It gets very busy here from four o'clock. Every station has a drive show, but it's news hourly and then headlines on the half-hour. I also work up to a 15-minute news programme at six o'clock.

Q   *What type of equipment are you using at the station?*

CH   Luckily, Huers [a type of old-fashioned tape recorder] are 'dying' now. They're so archaic and unreliable these days. When we go out to do interviews, we take mini-discs. We've got two belonging to the station, and then journalists have got their own. They're [the MDs] brilliant: small, diddy and excellent quality. We've also got a cassette recorder, just in case we've got to use it, but once you've used a mini-disc, you realize how great they are.

Q   *And what about editing equipment?*

CH   We've got a digital editing package called 'Audio Vault'. When it works, it's a fabulous system, but this station, along with a BBC national station are the only ones to use it in the UK. Other stations use 'Robert' or other more widely used systems. It's a very easy system once you get into it. We also use 'Sadie' which is a mixing package. All of our adverts are made up on Sadie.

Q *Have you ever gone out on assignment only to realize you've forgotten to replace the batteries in a recorder?*

CH The batteries are always powered; the discs we always check before we go. What was embarrassing was when I went to interview one of our MPs. They're all human, but they're quite important people and invariably they're on really short time limits. Anyway, I got all set up and started to ask questions, but there was nothing registering on the mini-disc. Yet all the attachment bits were up. I actually persuaded him to pop into the studio on his way to Westminster to do the interview again. The problem with the mini-disc turned out to be the smallest bit of rust had formed on the microphone socket, and being so sensitive, it wouldn't register.

Q *What about mistakes live on air?*

CH When I first started, it was the week the impeachment trial was beginning for President Clinton and it was also the week IRN was sending out package upon package about Princess Diana as it was about to come up to the first anniversary of her death. I spent all day taking all these different packages about Diana, also trying to keep up to date in the latter half of the afternoon when things were kicking off in America about President Clinton. My big feature at six o'clock – my first story – I opened the microphone and said, 'I'm Caroline Hodgson … Princess Clinton …' And I had to just carry on. I couldn't laugh, couldn't correct myself. The adrenalin pumping through your body takes over and you don't laugh. You don't get flummoxed or anything; you might skip a word, but carry on.

Q *Does the station supply you with a uniform of sorts when you're out reporting? Or does it expect you to adhere to a dress code?*

CH   I dress smartly anyway for myself. It is in our news guidelines that on occasion when we do have to go out, 'members of the public don't want to see someone who's scruffily dressed'. You don't have to wear a suit, but trousers or a skirt and blouse, or a top and jacket, that's the normal type of thing that's worn these days. We are given a polo shirt with the station emblem on it and a sweatshirt. We also have a big overcoat jacket with the station's emblem on it – which is really good for wet and windy days.

Q   *What are the station's rules? For example, is studio discipline strict?*

CH   Rules vary from department to department. I work to news guidelines – everything from local stories must be rewritten after three times on air so they don't sound stale; you can't use the word 'local' because the word doesn't mean local to everybody. Someone local to Bognor Regis isn't local to Midhurst. We weren't allowed to use sport in our main bulletin until the guidelines were revised. There are strict things that I have to work to such as law guidelines so you don't end up in court on a contempt charge.

Q   *To whom are you directly responsible?*

CH   My immediate boss is the news editor.

Q   *How do you find out what your assignments will be?*

CH   We've got a diary system. We do a lot of forward planning. I write up the following day's stories. So I invariably know in the morning when I listen to the morning bulletin, what the news is. If something new has cropped up, I can guess I'll be going out to get some reaction. You've got to have a 'handle' on things.

Q   *Do you keep a contacts book yourself?*

CH   Yes, one. Basically, every single person I'm in contact with, affecting my news day, will get logged in my contact book. I can't describe how important that is. If you think, Fred the butcher in the local village has spoken about the beef crisis, you must put his name in the book because you never know when you will need him again.

Q   *Did your course prepare you for writing news bulletins?*

CH   In the two years I've been here, my writing skills have
          improved twenty-fold. You learn as you go along. My news
          editor is a good teacher; he's very good at news.

Q   *Do you use a conventional PC to write your scripts?*

CH   I write my scripts on Word, but we'll be using 'Robert' soon.
          'Robert' actually puts the IRN script and your own script into
          the machine. It's easier because it times the piece for you and
          sorts out the audio.

Q   *Can you touch type?*

CH   No, but I'm pretty fast though.

Q   *Do you use shorthand?*

CH   I do. Not as much as I should, but you see I don't do any
          court reporting. That comes from the 'stringers' (freelance
          news correspondents). I jot things down from the wires to get
          stories.

Q   *Why aren't you reporting from the courts?*

CH   The station is so small that affording – time-wise or money-
          wise – to send somebody out to court is expensive. So
          freelance stringers file in copy and if it's a good case, you
          take it, which may be just half a dozen lines. They file copy
          for the newspapers and TV stations as well. Some news
          agencies specifically cover courts.

Q   *Have you done any vox pops or three-minute features?*

CH   I hate voxing. It's the worst thing in the world. I've done lots
          of features. We do fifteen-minute news programmes that go
          out three times a day, and we have features that are usually
          one and a half minutes long – sometimes longer – and they
          can either be wraps [packages] or two-ways.

Q   *Is all your work concerned with issues in West Sussex?*

CH   I was actually sent over to Northern Ireland for three days to
          do a piece on the disbanding of a Royal Military Police Unit,
          because of their connection with Chichester. That was a
          fantastic experience, going somewhere different, gathering

information and making the best of it when I got back. It was Easter and the time of the Good Friday Agreement, so something like that is tremendous, but it does not come around often. We've got a really rich news patch here with Goodwood and its Festival of Speed and the Motor Circuit Revival twice a year. The characters and celebrities you get here, the motor racing stars, the chance you have to put all that together and make programmes is unbelievable. It's right on your doorstep so we are lucky in that respect.

Q *How do you see your career developing?*

CH I'm taking a career break to get married. If I wasn't getting married, I'd be thinking about going to a bigger station as a senior reporter or going to a smaller one as a news editor. I like radio, but I've become quite disillusioned with the industry. Despite the fun, there are times when you pull your hair out and cry your eyes out. Working six days a week, and the wages are appalling. You don't do this for the money – certainly not in independent radio – you do it for the fun of it. Having put myself through a degree and a postgrad, and having to take out a loan of up to £10,000 to pay for that postgrad, only to be in a job where your starting salary is about £11,000. In over two years that's only risen by a £1,000 ... it's appalling. Yes, the BBC does pay more, but it's a completely different working environment.

Q *How many hours a week do you work? Forty ... fifty ... sixty hours?*

CH Sometimes more. My hours are supposed to be between 11 am to 7 pm. I'm never out of here at 7 o'clock – ever. Sometimes I'm in earlier; sometimes I stay later. And I work a Sunday generally. In these last two weeks, I started work on Monday at 5 o'clock in the morning and I've worked through all two weeks without a day off. To work 11 days on the trot for £38 a shift is not good.

Q *What is your holiday entitlement?*

CH Twenty days a year.

Q   *How much of your work is done from the newsroom, on the
          telephone?*

CH   It's a part of it, you phone people to ask questions, to arrange
          interviews, see what they're doing. You phone people like
          the coastguard, fire and ambulance to get your check calls.
          It's an extension of your writing hand, phoning people up for
          everything. Now we've got the Internet, you can use that for
          bits and bobs. You can tap into government press releases on
          housing, for instance.

Q   *Are you a member of a trade union?*

CH   I'm not a member because I can't afford to be. Which I think
          is sad. It would only cost something like £10 a month, but I
          cannot afford to do that.

Q   *Thank you.*

17 COURT REPORTING

This chapter outlines what is entailed in reporting legal cases and inquiries, but in no way does it attempt to provide a comprehensive account of court reporting.

Reporters intending to cover legal cases should ideally have passed a relevant examination as part of a course accredited by the NCTJ or BJTC.

The law and journalism

Journalists do not need to know every nuance of criminal law in the way a solicitor or barrister does. However, it is important that they know the laws affecting their roles as journalists: to know what can be reported, and what cannot.

The first thing to realize is that journalists in the UK along with all other citizens have access to enter and observe proceedings in 'all [the] courts of justice'. The presence of both press and public is to 'ensure that justice is done.' In these modern times, though, exceptions have been brought in to exclude the public from juvenile courts and domestic proceedings.

The press, unlike ordinary members of the public, have two advantages when attending court: the first is what is known as qualified privilege, which allows journalists to report any allegation or statement made in court without fear of libel. This does not apply to allegations or statements made outside the courtroom. Under common law and statute, the qualification stipulates that any reports must be 'fair, accurate and contemporaneous', meaning published in the first possible edition and not held back for any reason.

The second advantage is that journalists have their own seating set to one side of the court, though many reporters would complain this was no advantage especially in older court buildings where views are distant and proceedings difficult to hear.

No responsible editor sends a trainee or junior reporter alone to cover a court case as one of their first assignments. Even if the reporter has experience of covering courts as a journalism student, it would be a careless editor who allows them to cover a case alone; there is too much at stake and no newspaper can afford the risk of being fined for defamation or contempt of court.

Covering a case with a more experienced colleague is beneficial in more ways than one. Working with another reporter, you will learn how the paper receives notification of forthcoming cases. Sometimes, notices are displayed at the court, but only on the day of the hearings. Despite recommendations from the Home Office that papers should be notified as soon as lists are compiled, this does not always happen. Some papers estimate the approximate dates of criminal cases, having already covered the crime and arrest of the defendants. This is where a good rapport with the local police pays dividends as they may inform the paper of when a case is going to be heard. It is in the interest of the police to keep journalists informed, especially if publicity will aid further inquiries. Information may come from a desk sergeant, CID officers or by way of the force press office.

In respect of criminal hearings, the list provides details of the accused and the charge(s) against them under a specified Act and section. Other details include those of the arresting officer. Even if an entire police squad was present at the time of arrest, only the arresting officer is listed.

Inside the court, the journalist adheres to the same rules as any other member of the public, and sits silently throughout the proceedings. The journalist has no special privileges whilst the court is in session, but can approach the clerk to the court, solicitors or barristers, or the police who staff criminal courts once the court has been adjourned. Over time, when experience has been gained, clerks and ushers will recognize you and offer help where needs be. Under no circumstances is it possible to approach judges, magistrates or jurors.

The process of reporting events is similar to any other news event in that you make detailed notes of relevant information. However, it is of paramount importance that you note items correctly. The correct spelling of names and addresses with details in full, is crucial. You cannot list the defendant as simply 'John Smith of Smith Road, Smithtown', as there might be more than one John Smith resident in Smith Road. The defendant's full name and full address must be given with correct spelling. In your notebook, write names and addresses in upper case – always double-check spelling. If you need to check facts, do so with the clerk of the court.

You cannot use devices such as tape recorders or mini-discs (however small) in a courtroom, nor should you attempt to carry one into court concealed or otherwise. When taking notes, date your entries and title them appropriately: 'The Crown versus John Smith', or whatever. Be sure to keep all notes for at least six months in case of libel writs against you and the paper or for any other problem.

One final point on notes: they are valid only in their original form; transcribing them onto a computer disk or audio tape means they are no longer admissible records that can be used in a court of law.

The courts

In essence, there are four types of court in the British legal system: civil, criminal, appeal and coroners'courts.

Civil courts

Civil courts hear disputes – usually small claims – brought by individuals seeking redress over personal or property disputes, debt, wills, family law, and so on, and anything construed as coming under civil law. Civil courts include:

- **County courts** – these address disputes that come under civil law but are presided over by circuit and district judges.
- **The High Court** – when all else fails, cases are referred to the High Court of Justice in London. The

High Court judge sits alone without a jury except when hearing cases of wrongful arrest, slander, libel and malicious prosecution

Criminal courts

Criminal courts include:

- **Magistrates' courts** – these are where criminal cases begin, and are presided over by two or more magistrates (specially chosen local men and women from any background; magistrates are unpaid). In cities, the presiding magistrate sits alone in a full-time professional capacity and is known as a stipendiary magistrate.
- **Crown courts** – these try serious crimes. A jury of 12 lay people (randomly picked from the register of electors) are requested to hear the evidence put by prosecution and defence councils and return a majority verdict.
- **Central Criminal Court** (Old Bailey) – tries the most high-profile cases which might last for months.

Appeal courts

When a person is convicted of a crime, or a decision is made against them in a civil court, they are normally given the right to appeal. Procedures for appeal can be directed to the following courts:

- **The Court of Appeal** – comprises three judges sitting in the High Court. Cases are presented by counsel but reach the court only if new evidence concerning the original conviction has come to light, or a strong case is made to demonstrate the convicted person has served long enough in prison and is not likely to be a further danger to society.
- **House of Lords** – the House of Lords can decide appeals heard by five law lords, not the entire House.
- **The European Court of Justice** – the European Court is available to citizens of EU member states for

appeal cases, but only after the appeal procedure has been followed in the country that originally tried the case. Member countries agree to the Court's decisions, which are binding.

Coroners' court

The oldest office under the British Crown is that of the coroner, dating back over one thousand years. Coroners' courts differ in respect of their inquisitorial role; their purpose, chiefly, is to establish the cause of death and identity of the deceased where an occurrence of premature death means that a doctor will not sign a certificate for reasons of insufficient evidence relating to the cause of death. Although there are permanent coroners' offices, a coroner can use other buildings to conduct inquiries. The coroner is a part-time official, appointed from the profession of lawyer or doctor; their recommendations can result in significant safety changes. A coroner sitting with a jury returns a verdict; a coroner sitting alone records a verdict.

Who's who in court

- **Barristers** – not to be confused with solicitors, form the council for the prosecution (or defence) in crown courts. They have what the law calls 'the right to audience', that is to present and argue a case in all courts of law including magistrates' courts, the House of Lords and the European courts. Traditionally attired in gowns and wigs except in magistrates' courts.
- **Solicitors** – like barristers, solicitors have the right to audience. Unlike barristers, they represent lay clients in civil court actions as well as criminal court actions.

Books

Tom Crone, *Law and the Media* (3rd edition). Focal Press, 1995 Contents include: libel; the legal system; court reporting; journalist's sources; Official Secrets Act and D-notices; and much more.

18 | INTERNET JOURNALISM

As the first pages in the history of the Internet are still being written, any attempt to describe the job of a typical Internet journalist is, for now, not without its problems.

Since the arrival of online news sites in the mid-1990s, there has been considerable re-evaluation on the part of both print and broadcast media on the roles Internet journalism can and should deliver. Newspapers that had thought it would be enough simply to transfer their print pages to websites have had to rethink.

As television was to radio, and in its turn, radio to print, the Internet 'demands' to be recognized as a separate and unique entity. It might complement, but it is not a subtype of other media. It is not an electronic newspaper or freeze-framed TV screen.

There are plenty of paradoxes in the way the 'old guard' has harnessed the new medium, with the regional British press readily embracing the technology by putting 'local' news online. News normally intended for small populations of several thousand, can now reach global communities: a tractor engineer in Saskatchewan can keep abreast of gas main repairs in Melksham, Wiltshire.

Of course, the web is as relevant on a local level as it is on an international one and, irony aside, there is not a good reason why even a parish magazine should not harness its benefits to disseminate news and church service bulletins.

There is another irony: because of its accessibility, there is nothing to stop a journalist from working alone to create their own news site on the web and thus compete directly with the conglomerates who in other circumstances would be their employer. In this respect, Internet journalism allows the reporter to sidestep any attempt to constrict a newsgathering operation by those whose immense wealth or political power would normally have influenced content.

What undoubtedly *will* influence global and local newsgathering and dissemination is the consumer's ability to choose just what news they wish to see. Unlike television and radio news broadcasts where the listener or viewer is passive, by using special devices – agents – to search the web, the consumer will be able to select just what type of news is relevant to them. This might at first suggest that the consumer will filter out the famines, wars and disasters in favour of lifestyle features, sport, competitions and entertainment.

According to Jim Hall in his book, *Online Journalism: A Critical Primer,* companies such as America On Line (AOL) already see their role as 'news packagers' rather than gatherers, with no place for the journalist. Yet, as Hall goes on to point out, the demand for news from those using the Internet immediately following the death of Diana Princess of Wales in 1997, rose by 'more than 600 per cent over that of the previous weekend', clearly demonstrating that 'packaging' could never in itself be a substitute for newsgathering.

Interview with Daniel Garrett

Daniel Garrett writes and maintains a website for the Swindon-based *Evening Advertiser* and *Devizes Gazette and Herald* newspapers. He also writes an Internet column for the *Devizes Gazette and Herald* in which he reviews websites.

Q   *How did you begin working as an Internet journalist?*

DG   I used to work for a website company and learnt a lot of the technical aspects of the Net and computers in general. I always had an interest in web design and I was designing sites alongside working in a technical role. A position came up for a web designer-cum-webmaster for my local paper the *Evening Advertiser*, where I am now. I applied because it was something I wanted to move into and was based on my experience. I actually had to design a website for my interview, and on the strength of some of the ideas that I brought forward, I was given the job. I've always been pretty good at English and had a great interest in words and reading. That naturally applied itself to editing and [writing] online. I write an editorial for the newspaper as well as online pages related to what's happening on the Internet.

Q   *Do you have any training or qualifications as a journalist?*

DG None at all.

Q   *What subjects are the paper's web pages covering?*

DG On the Internet we do a page called 'This is Wiltshire'. We upload all the relevant news and sport, and information that goes into the newspaper. Whenever there's something going into the paper that requires somebody with a bit of Internet knowledge to comment on, then they usually ask me to write something. We recently did a 32-page supplement for all our titles in Wiltshire and for that I wrote a piece on buying over the Internet and downloading music from the Internet, as well as an overview of our site. I also write on a regular basis for 'This is Wiltshire' which is a round-up of picks of the week. That goes online as well as in the *Devizes Gazette and Herald* every week.

Q   *When a reporter files copy, do they upload the copy to an ftp (file transer protocol) file you can access?*

DG It doesn't really come to me; it comes up automatically. They [reporters] only have a limited amount of time to check each character is going to be displayed perfectly on the Internet. For example, they might include an instruction that says, 'continued on page 2'. Well, that doesn't mean anything on the Internet, so you have to proofread it quickly.

Q   *What advice would you give to an aspirant Internet journalist?*

DG Have something that you can show to a prospective employer like a website you've already done. That will go a long way on your CV to improving your chances. Don't worry too much about going to university. Because it's such a new industry, experience is just as important.

Q   *Did you go to university?*

DG No. I've got about three GCSEs. It isn't a true reflection on ability, I don't think.

Q *What web design tool do you work with?*

DG We use Dreamweaver, Photoshop, Paintshop Pro. The editorial team use QuarkXpress and Power Collector, which enables them to format the news to go on to the website fairly easily. The journalists generally use Macs but we're mainly PC-based here.

Q *You use PCs for design work?*

DG Yes, because it doesn't have to be such a high resolution for the Internet because of the download time. The file sizes need to be fairly small so it's not important if you've got thousands of RAM because you're doing a 600 dpi [dots per inch] image.

Q *What sort of response are you getting from people 'hitting' the site?*

DG A great response. We'll be revamping the site shortly. There is a little pop-up window that comes up when you go to 'This is Wiltshire' that will take you to what the new site will look like. It also asks you a few quick questions about what you like or what you don't like. People are very interactive with us on a regular basis through all the different things that are on the web page like, 'Where are they now?' and 'Swindon Town Football Club'; that sort of thing.

Q *Do you get responses from people around the world?*

DG Quite a few. That goes in the 'Where are they now?' section. People writing to say that they moved out of Wiltshire or Swindon and they want to get in contact with old friends. And there have been a couple of success stories there.

Q *Thank you.*

Surfing the Net

Checkout the 'Online Journalism Review' at http://www.ojr.usc.edu
Also Journalism Forum: The Online Press Club at
http://www.jforum.org

Books

Jim Hall, *Online Journalism: A Critical Primer*. Pluto Press, 2000

19 | SPECIALIST PRESS

Over the past two decades there has been a significant expansion in the specialist press. At the beginning of the twenty-first century there is a plethora of small presses publishing magazines and newspapers for companies in-house and online in the UK. The range of subjects covered is as varied as the companies' products. Some are promotional magazines aimed at customers visiting supermarkets and large stores; others produce purely in-house newspapers and magazines for their staff. The contents consist of news and informative articles for staff members, keeping them abreast of events in their industry. These are not amateur publications written and printed to a 'parish magazine' format. Indeed, professional staff and freelance journalists are employed by the company to produce the publication, and consequently there are openings for those with the right skills.

Focus on *Wessex Water News*

Wessex Water supplies public water services to Bristol, Bath, Somerset, Dorset and Wiltshire. The company publishes two magazines, *Customer News* and *Wessex Water News*, for its employees. Topics are mainly concerned with the water industry and include news and features on world, national and regional developments. There is a strong emphasis on environmental issues (rivers, lakes and their wildlife), and staff developments such as promotions, awards, achievements, retirements, obituaries and special events. There is no commercial advertising.

Wessex Water News is online at www.wessexwater.co.uk

Interview with Ian Martin

The following interview is with writer and consultant, Ian Martin, 29 of *Wessex Water News*, one of two in-house magazines produced by the water services company Wessex Water. Ian was a reporter for various weekly and evening newspapers before entering public relations. Prior to joining Wessex Water he was assistant editor of another staff newspaper.

Q   *Did you begin your journalistic career in trade/specialist journalism?*

IM   No, I started in regional journalism working for a weekly newspaper.

Q   *Did you always want to be a journalist?*

IM   I had wanted to become a journalist since I was 11 years old.

Q   *Did you train to become a journalist, and if so, where?*

IM   I did a one-year journalism course run by the National Council for the Training of Journalists before doing two years as a trainee on a weekly newspaper.

Q   *Is* Wessex Water News *considered to be a trade paper or specialist paper?*

IM   It is an employee newspaper which aims to keep existing and retired staff informed about news and developments within the company.

Q   *When was the paper first produced?*

IM   The paper was first published in the 1970s.

Q   *Do you use freelance contributions, and if so, how much of the paper do they constitute?*

IM   No, the paper is written entirely in-house.

Q   *How many people put the paper together?*

IM   The paper is written and subbed by the editor and the design is carried out by our in-house designer.

Q   *How do you think the paper will develop?*

IM In January 2000, *Wessex Water News* was relaunched as an intranet newspaper by the team in-house. A redesigned A4 news magazine is produced monthly and sent to staff who do not have access to the Intranet.

Q *How is the paper funded?*

IM The paper is funded out of the budget allocated to Wessex Water's public relations department.

Q *How is the paper distributed?*

IM The intranet version is available online. The paper version is posted to key people at each location who then distribute it manually.

Q *Approximate circulation figures?*

IM Circa 3,000.

Q *If you were employing a journalist to work on* Wessex Water News, *what personal qualities, education and experience would you be looking for?*

IM They would need several years' experience in newspaper journalism, excellent writing skills, good interpersonal and communication skills and lots of ideas. Knowledge of the water industry would be a distinct advantage.

Q *What advice would you give to aspirant journalists wishing to work in the specialist press?*

IM Persevere. Entering journalism is very difficult and requires determination because there are a lot of people wishing to enter the profession. If you specialize, a good knowledge of the industry you wish to join would be an advantage. Read as many newspapers and publications as you can because this will help you to learn about the various writing styles used in different publications as well as giving you an overview of the various publications produced.

Q *Thank you.*

20 | TRADE UNION MEMBERSHIP

Whether you become a staff or freelance journalist and work as either a reporter, writer, copywriter, subeditor, photographer, researcher, broadcaster, presenter, press officer, illustrator, or any one of a host of related professions, membership of a trade union is to be recommended. In the UK, unions such as the NUJ (National Union of Journalists), the Chartered Institute of Journalists and the British Association of Journalists, work hard to provide a bedrock of support for their members.

During a journalist's career, there will almost certainly come a time when union support is sought. By the very nature of journalism, with its frequent reporting of criminal proceedings, long hours spent working at a desk and, for some, frequent travel abroad, there are bound to be problems – small or large.

Disputes can easily arise out of working conditions:

- Health problems caused through working long hours at a computer – a problem that affects many subeditors.
- Malpractice on the part of employers – trainee journalists working long hours without supervision and without pay.
- The capture and imprisonment of journalists working abroad.

These are just some of the many problems encountered by journalists that the unions will take up on behalf of their members.

Case study

When journalist John McCarthy was captured and held hostage by Islamic Jihad in Beirut, 1986, his then girlfriend, Jill Morrell, began a campaign to keep his name alive in the minds of the public and politicians. Together with friends and colleagues, Jill was determined that people should not forget the plight of John and the other hostages and knew that the only way to do this was convince the media that the hostages were still news even though little was known of their fate. However, as the tempo of the campaign increased, it became necessary to find an office from which The Friends of John McCarthy – all volunteers – could operate: a telephone and address were vital. Jill approached the NUJ for help. The union promptly found them an office and circulated requests to all members asking them to include news of John in their reports; a petition was also organized among members which was then delivered to Downing Street and the Iranian Embassy. The office – part of the NUJ's main offices – enabled the Friends to base their campaign centrally in London. In addition, self-motivated union members organised their own events to raise money and awareness.

The unions are not just there for life's difficult situations. Regular social meetings and advice are always available, whether it is in connection with what PC to buy, how to avoid repetitive strain injury or what sort of training is required to enter the profession or improve existing skills.

National Union of Journalists

The NUJ is the largest of the three unions and a member of both the National Council for the Training of Journalists (NCTJ) and the Broadcast Journalism Training Council (BJTC). Although not directly involved in the training of students, it makes sure that all aspirant journalists are trained properly and fairly.

Students on NUJ-approved training courses can join as temporary members without paying membership fees. This free membership continues for the first three months of employment.

Freelance members, like their staff colleagues, receive an NUJ press card and advice on freelance issues such as copyright and money matters, among many other things. There are even special deals on insurance, loans and mortgages. In the early stages of building up a freelance career, journalists can apply for temporary membership providing that journalism is their main career and they can provide evidence of recently published work. Freelance members receive a fees guide and can register their names and skills in the union's Freelance Directory.

The Chartered Institute of Journalists

The Chartered Institute of Journalists (CIoJ) is the oldest journalist organization in the world, having been founded in 1884. Queen Victoria granted the Institute a royal charter in 1890. Members meet annually and may use the letters MCIJ after their name; fellows may use FCIJ.

The Institute has two roles: that of professional organization – CIoJ – the other as trade union – IoJ(TU). Members hold a press card and 'newsgatherers' card', and, like NUJ members, benefit from representation, guidance and advice. Regular journals keep members informed, and discounts are offered on certain services.

CIoJ is a constitute member of the NCTJ which in turn gives its members a voice on the Council as well as the British Copyright Council, the British Photographic Liaison Committee, and the Campaign for Freedom of Information.

Applicants are eligible to join as either a full member, student member or affiliate member.

For the contact book

The Chartered Institute of Journalists
2 Dock Offices
Surrey Quays Road
London SE16 2XU
Tel: 020 7252 1187
Fax: 020 7232 2302
E-mail: memberservice@ioj.co.uk

National Union of Journalists
Acorn House
314, Gray's Inn Road
London WC1X 8DP
Tel: 020 7278 7916
Fax: 020 7837 8143
E-mail: NUJ@mcr1.poptel.org.uk
Internet: www.nuj.org.uk

21 | THE JOURNALIST AS SOLDIER

Serving members of the Territorial Army's Media Operations Group are volunteer soldiers who also happen to have regular jobs in journalism and public relations. Media Operations is a growing and demanding role as conflicts around the world escalate and United Nations and NATO members commit troops for various peacekeeping operations.

Not all Media Operations Group personnel operate from the various war zones. The essential work of the unit is to take the everyday news and events of army life and despatch stories to the press, regional TV and local radio stations. These are human interest stories of both regular and territorial Army personnel serving at home or abroad, and they provide a vital link for the soldiers' families and friends.

Media v. military

Army commanders recognize the need to take the media into consideration when planning military strategy. The army has a constitutional and legal obligation to inform the public of 'activities undertaken on their behalf'. This is not a new idea: armies throughout the ages have had to gain, maintain and increase the support of those left at home. Information is important not only to the 'home side' of families, friends and fellow citizens of those serving, but to international communities and even the host nation – which might include the enemy. For some countries, the only information available may be from the armed forces of the powers attempting to resolve a conflict.

The deployment of international soldiers to any one of the world's trouble spots is big news throughout the world. Media coverage of the conflicts in the Gulf, Bosnia, Somalia, Haiti, the Balkans and East Timor has grown over the years with each successive operation. During the Gulf War in 1991, there were over 1,500 journalists in 'the field' with the military.

In the past, both journalists and military accepted that an 'undeclared' state of war existed between them – despite the remarkable journalistic coverage of the Second World War which was so vital in recording events for families at home and future generations. Quite understandably, the military insists that secrecy is essential in a war zone. Yet the armies of democratic countries are also directly answerable to their elected governments. This is where the media demands its right to know and inform. Also, today's soldiers are themselves members of a generation brought up on the mass media: television, radio and the press. All ranks of the modern army go home to put the TV on or surf the Net, just like anybody else. Everyone has a need to be informed and will expect a democratic society to provide that information.

However, in recent years, the realization that mutual co-operation benefits both camps is one that is increasingly accepted thanks to greater communication between the two. The accepted understanding now is that the media's need to know does not necessarily jeopardize a military operation. Indeed, international news coverage of wars can in themselves destroy the enemy's propaganda claims in the face of defeat. Television broadcasts and Internet journalism recognize no boundaries, making it very difficult for a dictator or totalitarian government to claim the advantage if they are losing.

It is because of technology in the form of satellite up-links, mobile telephones and laptop computers connected to the Internet that the media has released itself from dependency on military-controlled transmissions. Pundits suggest that, in future conflicts, the media will be able to run a newsgathering and information operation parallel with that of the military, so a degree of co-operation is inevitable.

In this respect, the necessity to foster an understanding between media and military is well met by the Media Operations Group and Reservist Public Affairs Branch of the Royal Navy and Royal Air Force Volunteer Reserve.

Media Operations Group personnel can provide an important bridge between the regular army and the media. As Territorial Army soldiers, they are civilians with regular civilian jobs. Although just over one-quarter of the group's personnel are ex-forces, the remainder come from a purely civilian background and are employed in television, radio, the national press and public relations. Writers, broadcasters, photographers and linguists, they bring a wide range of talents to army/media relations.

The Media Operations Group

Yesterday and today

Originally known from its formation in the 1970s as TAPIO (Territorial Army Pool of Public Information Officers) the unit was renamed the Media Operations Group (V) in September 1996 (now known as G3 Media Operations Group). The few times that group personnel gather together are three weekends a year and an annual camp. As part of their commitment, personnel are sent on operational taskings and training taskings. They assist with exercises and operational training that includes regular and TA training.

The Media Operations Group is not a regiment or company in its own right: it is a specialist independent unit. All the unit's personnel enter the service after initial officer training and begin their service as commissioned officers with the rank of captain. They wear the uniform and cap badge of the regiment to which they have chosen to be assigned. Some applicants come to the unit direct from service in the regular army or other TA units.

Tomorrow

Applicants to the G3 Media Operations Group should bear in mind that these are not part-time posts for war correspondents. The unit's officers are carefully selected at a selection board held over two days, with all candidates, including those applying from the regular army and other TA units, undergoing selection. If candidates are considered suitable, they will be given a place in the unit. As with all the armed forces, the TA requires disciplined individuals who can learn to operate in the field as a soldier as well as a journalist. In other words, before you volunteer, you will need to have a high degree of physical and mental fitness. Amongst other things, you will be trained to shoot pistols as well as cameras, undertake a combat fitness test, understand military media campaign planning, media operations, and commit yourself to a readiness to stand alongside your TA and regular army comrades at any time.

Travel is one of the perks of the job. Personnel can volunteer to mobilize and take part in exercises for a period between three and six months. Before applying, you must make sure that your regular employer, partner and family understand the part-time commitment that is required.

Further information

Contact your nearest Territorial Army office.

INDEX